For Sale By Owner: A Complete Guide

STEVE BERGES

McGraw-Hill

New York   Chicago San Francisco Lisbon London
Madrid Mexico City Milan New Delhi San Juan
Seoul Singapore Sydney Toronto

The *McGraw·Hill* Companies

1 2 3 4 5 6 7 8 9 0   DOC/DOC   0 9 8 7 6 5

ISBN 0-07-145825-5

This publication is designed to provide accurate and authoritative information in regard to the subject matter covered. It is sold with the understanding that neither the author nor the publisher is engaged in rendering legal, accounting, or other professional service. If legal advice or other expert assistance is required, the services of a competent professional person should be sought.

—From a declaration of principles jointly adopted by a committee of the American Bar Association and a committee of publishers

McGraw-Hill books are available at special quantity discounts to use as premiums and sales promotions, or for use in corporate training programs. For more information, please write to the Director of Special Sales, McGraw-Hill Professional, Two Penn Plaza, New York, NY 10121-2298. Or contact your local bookstore.

 This book is printed on recycled, acid-free paper containing a minimum of 50% recycled, de-inked fiber.

Library of Congress Cataloging-in-Publication Data

Berges, Steve.
    For sale by owner : a complete guide / by Steve Berges.— 1st ed.
       p.   cm.
    Includes index.
    ISBN 0-07-145825-5 (alk. paper)
    1. House selling. 2. Real property. I. Title.
  HD1379.B427 2006

  643'.12'068—dc22   2005017824

Contents

Contents

Contents

Contents

PART I

The FSBO's Home Preparation Checklist

1

Selling Your House: The Difference between Success and Failure

Introduction

According to the National Association of Realtors, greater than expected sales of existing homes in 2004 set an all-time record for annual sales. Existing home sales for 2004 increased approximately 6.5 percent over 2003, bringing the total to slightly more than 6.78 million houses. Of these, approximately 15 percent were sold directly by their owners, rather than through a real estate agency. This means that over 1 million homes were sold as *for sale by owner*, or *FSBO*. Estimates indicate that, in addition to the homes that actually sold as FSBOs, approximately 750,000 more homeowners attempted to sell their homes without the aid of a real estate agent, bringing the total number of those who sold and those who attempted to sell FSBO to about 1.75 million households. This data suggests that, while slightly more than half of all homeowners who attempted to sell their own houses did so, slightly less than half did not.

The question that naturally arises is, "What was it that made the difference between those homeowners who succeeded in selling their own houses and those who did not?" The answer is information. There are several key variables that affect the marketability of any house. These variables include the condition of the property, its price and location, the availability and terms of financing, the advertising channels used to market the property, and, perhaps most important of all, the seller's ability to manage the sales process from start to finish. Individuals selling their own houses must be capable of assessing the physical condition of their houses and determining which of all the improvements that can be made will improve the salability of the house. Homeowners must also understand how a comparative market analysis is done and how to find the proper balance between price and all other factors that may have an impact on the value of the home. The FSBOs must also be able to implement a broad and aggressive marketing campaign in order to bring potential buyers through to view their homes. The FSBO must furthermore be capable of showing and selling the important features and benefits of his or her house; using closing techniques to get an offer; and negotiating the price, terms, and conditions of the transaction. Finally, FSBOs must be able to manage the closing process and see it through to the end by working with key third-party businesses.

A lack of knowledge or understanding of any one of these important variables can mean the difference between success and failure for the FSBO. For example, if a FSBO sets the price of her house too high relative to the market she is selling in, there's a good chance the house will not sell. A comprehensive understanding of how to do a comparative market analysis, however, would alleviate that problem. Remember that price is only one of several variables that define the fragile balance between success and failure. Assuming the FSBO in this example sets the price of her house correctly, but has absolutely no knowledge of the sales process or how to work with buyers, then once again, the result is likely to be failure.

This book is intended to help people just like you to overcome the challenge of selling a house without the assistance of a real estate agent. In order to do that, however, you must not only arm yourself with knowledge, but also be prepared to act on that knowledge once it is obtained. Part I of this book focuses on the steps sellers must consider as they prepare to put their houses on the market for sale. Chapters 2 and 3 include comprehensive sections on low-cost, high-impact home improvements, both interior and exterior, that are designed to help FSBOs sell their homes for maximum profit in minimum time. Chapter 4 discusses the importance of understanding value, how to do a comparative market analysis, and the sensitive balance between price and time. Finally, Chapter 5 provides an in-depth look at 10 different forms used by sellers, some of which are essential to every real estate transaction, and others that are needed only in certain circumstances. For instance, while the sales contract and the seller's disclosure forms are essential to every transaction, other forms, such as third-party financing addendums, may only be needed occasionally.

While Part I explores the universe of home preparation, Part II provides an in-depth examination of marketing, selling, negotiating, and writing up the sales agreement. Part II begins with Chapter 6 and discusses seven different marketing techniques homeowners can use to gain maximum exposure for their houses. It includes an exhaustive section on strategic marketing and advertising initiatives with specific attention given not only to traditional methods of selling, but also to more advanced methods, such as how to take advantage of various Internet resources available to FSBOs. The more people who know your house is for sale, the better your chances are of getting it sold quickly and at the price you want. Chapter 7 discusses the advantages of using discount brokerage services and fee-for-service agents to gain even greater exposure for your house. Chapter 8 is intended to help FSBOs learn how to set appointments and show their houses to potential buyers, but only after taking certain safety precautions. Chapter 9 contains important information that will help sellers better understand the motives of the buyers they are working with. The better you understand the needs of a buyer, the better you will be able to negotiate with him or her. Once you and the buyer have reached an agreement, it is then time to formalize it by putting it in writing. Chapter 10 contains a complete step-by-step guide for filling out a sales contract, or purchase agreement, as it is also known.

After finding a buyer and writing up a purchase agreement, it's time to begin preparing for the closing. Part III walks the FSBO through the steps required to see the sale through all the way to the closing. It begins with Chapter 11, a comprehensive section about title insurance and how to select the best title company. The chapter is designed to inform you about title companies and the various services offered by them, alert you to some of the pitfalls to be aware of when working with a title company, help you to identify a competent title company in your area, and, finally, learn how to have the buyer pay for all or part of these services. Chapter 12 examines the home inspection process and what sellers can do to protect themselves against future litigation, regardless of whether or not a home inspection is done. Another important element of the sales process is the appraisal. Chapter 13 not only discusses the various types of appraisals, but also explains important differences between an appraisal and a comparative market analysis, as well as a broker's price opinion. Once the third party reports such as the home inspection, appraisal, and survey have been completed, it's time to prepare for the actual closing. Chapter 14 provides an exhaustive section about the importance of working with the title company and the buyer, understanding settlement statements and the various charges both buyers and sellers are customarily responsible for, and, finally, the closing itself. Long before the sale is completed, both the seller and the buyer must begin making moving preparations. Chapter 15 provides helpful information to FSBOs that will enable them to plan their moves without getting ahead of themselves.

By the time you've finished reading Parts I, II, and III of this book, you'll have a complete understanding of what it takes to sell your own house. Although you probably already realize there's more to selling a house than sticking a sign in the front yard, you'll gain an even greater appreciation for the process as a whole. You'll learn about the important steps required to prepare your house before ever placing it on the market. You'll learn how to price it correctly, how to market and show it to prospective buyers, how to negotiate with them, and how to write up a purchase agreement. Finally, you'll learn about the necessary steps required to ensure that the title work is done correctly, that all third-party reports are completed when they should be, and what it takes to close the sale. By applying the information contained in this book, you'll be able to sell your house for the maximum amount of profit in the minimum amount of time possible!

The FSBO's Goals and Objectives

Now that we've discussed what this book is about, let's take a moment to review your goals. The primary objective for most homeowners who place their houses on the market for sale is to get their houses sold as close to full market value as possible. The timing for sellers, of course, varies by the degree of urgency and is often reflected in price. While some homeowners are in no hurry whatsoever to sell, others need to sell as quickly as possible. Price therefore becomes a function of time, at least in part. A secondary objective for many homeowners, especially those desiring to sell their own houses, is to save money in the process so as to minimize the cost of selling and thereby maximize the net return to them.

If homeowners can achieve both of the stated objectives at the same time, then so much the better. The trade-off in this process, however, is the substitution of labor. All of the steps necessary to sell a house successfully don't go away just because you've decided to sell your house on your own. The work must still be done by someone, and that someone is you. Selling a house on your own to save money is no different from mowing your own lawn to save money. You can either hire a full service landscaping company to maintain the lawn for you and pay whatever the going rate is, or you can do it yourself and save money in the process. Regardless of how your lawn gets mowed, some form of service or labor is required and must be performed by someone. So the question becomes, "Are you willing to assume the many responsibilities assumed by the typical real estate agent to sell your own house, or would you rather pay the typical real estate agent for his or her services?" Only you, of course, can answer that question. If you are in no hurry to sell, you can always give it a try on your own and then, after a month or two goes by and you decide that perhaps you don't have the time or the inclination to sell your house after all, you still have the option of listing it with an agent.

The FSBO's Self-Assessment Checklist

Before attempting to sell your own house, you should not only consider the advantages and disadvantages of doing so, but also take stock of your own skill sets. In other words, by doing a self-assessment of your abilities and com-

The FSBO's Home Preparation Checklist

paring them to what it takes to get a house sold, you can determine whether you should sell your house on your own or hire a real estate agent to help you. Take a moment now to review the FSBO self-assessment checklist.

- [ ] Do I have to have a real estate license to sell my own home?

  To begin with, no, you do not have to have a special license to sell your own house, so you don't have to worry about preparing for a test or taking an exam. Anyone can sell their own house if they choose.

- [ ] Do I have the time to sell my own home?

  Perhaps the biggest issue in selling your own house is the amount of time you have to spend doing so. From start to finish, demands will be placed on you that will require your time. If you are busy working overtime, as well as nights and weekends, you may want to think seriously about having an agent help you. Buyers can be impatient, especially if they happen to be out driving on the weekend and spot your house. Agents will often drop everything to show a house to a buyer. If you're at work or have other commitments, you may not be able to respond as quickly as an agent. Showing your house is not the only demand placed on your time. Other commitments include preparing ads, distributing flyers, screening buyers, setting appointments, and working with an attorney or a title agent, to name but a few. If, on the other hand, you have ample time for these responsibilities, then by all means, go for it!

- [ ] Do I have the money to sell my own home?

  Another factor to consider when selling your own house is setting up a budget for advertising it. When a house is listed with a real estate agent, the agent picks up the tab for the marketing and advertising. When a homeowner sells her own house, however, she is responsible for those costs. Once again, it's a trade-off of resources. Either you pay an agent a commission to sell your house and advertise it, or you save the money from the commission and be prepared to pay for the advertising yourself.

- [ ] Do I know enough about marketing and advertising to sell my own home?

Selling Your House

Setting up an advertising budget is one thing. Knowing how best to use it is another. Marketing your house involves much more than just running an ad in the paper. To be successful in today's competitive environment, sellers must take advantage of as many advertising mediums as is practical. This means sellers must be prepared to launch an aggressive, multidimensional marketing campaign that will capture the attention of as many buyers as possible.

☐ Do I feel safe showing my home to strangers?

Sadly enough, this is a very real topic of concern, especially for women. Although there are certain safety precautions that can be taken to help minimize the degree of risk to the FSBO, there are no guarantees. If you intend to sell your house by owner, you must be prepared to deal with this very real issue.

☐ Am I comfortable enough with other people to be able to show and sell my house?

There is much more to selling your house than walking from room to room and saying, "This is the kitchen. This is the family room. This is the bedroom." In order to sell a house, you must be able to sell all the things you like about it to prospective buyers. The master salesperson knows how to present a house in its absolute, most favorable light. He knows how to put just the right spin on a room or feature of a house to make the buyer's mouth water. The master salesperson is not deceitful, but chooses to focus on the positive rather than the negative. He knows how to overcome the negative aspects of a house by accentuating the positive aspects. The master salesperson knows how to point out the features of a house and how to describe to the buyer how they will benefit her. Finally, the master salesperson knows when to talk and when to be quiet and really listen to what the buyer is saying. As a FSBO, you must be comfortable showing and selling your house to others.

☐ Do I have the necessary skills to interact and negotiate with buyers?

To *negotiate* means to confer with another person or party until such time as both parties have reached a mutual agreement or acceptance of a condition. To negotiate with a buyer requires that you have the ability to communicate effectively without getting your feathers ruffled. It's very easy to take offense to a comment made by the buyer because, after all, this is *your* house. You must be able to look beyond such remarks politely and professionally, all the while leading the buyer closer to your true objective of getting your house sold.

☐ Am I capable of reading and understanding legal documents?

Selling your own house also involves being able to read and understand the various legal documents that are necessary to complete a sales transaction. If you are not at all familiar with contracts, you can always enlist the aid of an attorney or a title agent who is familiar with them. On the other hand, if you have owned and sold a house in the past, you are already familiar with the process and should therefore have no problem understanding these documents.

☐ Do I know how to manage the closing process?

Managing the closing process primarily involves working with either an attorney or a title company, or both, to successfully complete the sale of your home. In order to ensure as smooth a closing as possible, there are several steps that must be taken prior to the actual date of the closing. They include scheduling a closing date with the buyer and the title company, providing the title company with updated mortgage information, and coordinating your move-out date with the buyer's move-in date. You can also prepare yourself for the closing by becoming familiar with the settlement statement and the various charges that buyers and sellers are customarily responsible for. Although the closing process is fairly straightforward, you must nevertheless be familiar with the steps involved to sell your house successfully.

The items listed in the FSBO self-assessment checklist are all covered in this book and can be learned by most anyone. The main question for most people who are deciding whether or not to sell their own houses is the amount of time they have to devote to this process. In other words, they must be willing to substitute their own labor for that of a real estate agent. Selling a house doesn't happen over a single weekend. Even in the best market, selling a house will take at least several weeks. In moderate to slow markets, selling a house can take several months, and even up to a year or more. Your awareness of and acceptance of the time it takes to sell a house is an important factor in the decision to sell your own house. If you believe that you have the time to devote to this process, then it's time to read on! Remember that the difference between success and failure when selling your own house is information. As you read and study the remainder of this book, you'll learn about all those elements that are essential to selling your house successfully, thereby allowing you to join the ranks of the 1 million plus people who do so every year!

2

Exterior Home Preparation: How to Make Low Cost, High Impact Improvements That Will Sell Your Home Fast

One of the most important things you can do when preparing to sell your home is to make sure that it is in good condition. This includes the home's exterior and interior appearance, as well as its overall functionality. In *101 Cost-Effective Ways to Improve the Value of Your Home* (Chicago: Dearborn Trade, 2004), I devised an impact value rating system, which is used to make generalizations about the value of various improvements to a home. This value system was designed to help homeowners make improvements to their houses that would add the most value for the least amount of money. Because the value of improvements varies widely by region, it is difficult to devise a system to rate them that would apply equally in all markets. What we can do, however, is devise a system based upon generalizations. Calculating an exact dollar amount for the value of an improvement is difficult, if not impossible, to do because there are so many factors that influence value. For example, an outdoor swimming pool would be worth more to a prospective buyer in a southern state such as Florida than it would be to a buyer in a northern state such as Maine; conversely, a high-efficiency furnace would be worth more to a prospective buyer in Maine than it would be to a buyer in Florida. The rating system I devised provides only general indications of value because of regional differences such as those just described. It is based on a scale of five stars, with one star having the lowest impact on value, three stars having a neutral impact on value, and five stars having the strongest impact on value. Although this chapter is by no means as comprehensive as *101 Cost-Effective Ways to Improve the Value of Your Home*, it does focus on some of the most important elements of home repair and home improvement that will help you get top dollar for your house.

Visibility Adds Value

One of the key factors emphasized in my home improvement book is the principle that *visibility adds value*. This notion centers on the idea that that the more visible an improvement is, the greater its worth to the resale value of a house. In other words, it embodies the intention of allowing a home-owner to get the greatest "bang for the buck" on various types of home improvements. Allow me to share a simple example with you. Although spending $7,500 on repairing a cracked foundation slab may be required to get a house sold, the repair itself is barely visible (if at all) and does nothing to improve the appearance of a house. On the other hand, spending the same $7,500 on improving the landscaping, installing new kitchen cabinets, and painting the interior of a house has a potentially much greater return for the same amount of dollars invested. This is because these improvements are all highly visible and will greatly enhance the beauty of the home. It's all about aesthetics. People tend to buy what they "see." In general, home improvements that have a greater propensity to improve the appearance of a home will realize a greater return than an equal amount of money spent on a repair that does nothing to improve a house's appearance. Keep the *visibility adds value* principle at the forefront of your mind as you begin preparing your home for resell. Making improvements based on this principle will enable you to maximize the resell value of your home while minimizing the cost to do so.

The Berges Yikes-Appeal Scale

Have you ever gone shopping for a house, pulled up in front of it, and exclaimed, "Yikes!"? I certainly have, and on more than one occasion. As an avid investor in foreclosed properties, I've looked at many houses that the average buyer would not even bother to stop at because of their exterior appearances. The Berges Yikes-Appeal Scale can best be likened to the scale used to rank the strength of hurricanes. If there is no hurricane, then there is no rating. Only if a hurricane exists is there a rating assigned. While a category one hurricane can pose a serious threat, it is not nearly as dangerous or destructive as a category five hurricane. Similarly, a house in good condition with an inviting and welcoming appearance does not register on the Berges Yikes-Appeal Scale. Only when a house's condition warrants a "Yikes" reaction is it assigned a rating. A house having a category one yikes rating, for example, is not nearly as foreboding and uninviting as a house having a category five rating.

I've seen, walked through, and even purchased houses with yikes appeal ratings across the entire spectrum of the yikes–appeal rating system. Those houses that I would assign a category five to have had walls and doors kicked in, windows smashed, floors trashed, furnaces and air conditioning components removed or stolen, basements flooded, and trees and shrubs greatly overgrown. I've also been through houses where the stench from animal urine and feces was so strong that I wondered aloud if the house had quite possibly been the subject of a chemical or biological attack. Believe it or not though, I actually prefer these types of deals because I know average buyers will run the other way as soon as they open the door. The immediate attack on the olfactory and visual senses strengthened by the impact of the sometimes frightening appearance of these houses is enough to scare most buyers away.

Think about your own experiences for a moment. Let's say, for example, you're out looking at houses one day and have 10 on your list to look at. If you pull up to one that looks like it hasn't seen a fresh coat of paint in 25 years, has beer cans scattered about, and has motorcycles parked in the front yard, there's a good chance you'll keep right on driving. A house has to be inviting from the outside before a potential buyer will even bother to stop and look at the inside. An unkempt appearance on the outside is a good indicator of a house's appearance on the inside. It's no different from shopping at a retail discount store. If there are two items side by side that are identical, with the exception that one is in a package that has been damaged because it was dropped on the floor and the other one sits neatly on the shelf in a package that has not been damaged, which one would you choose? Unless the item in the damaged package was offered at a significant discount, you would most likely choose the item in the undamaged package. Be sure your house looks like it's in an undamaged package and that it doesn't register on the Berges Yikes-Appeal Scale!

Is the Outside of Your House Bright and Cheery, or Dark and Dreary?

There was a period of time during the 1970s when it was common practice to paint newly constructed housing a dark brown color. To this day, I can't figure out why dark brown was so popular, but, for whatever reason, it was. Dark colors in general create an uninviting appearance, especially dark brown. In addition, if a house is surrounded by lots of shrubs and overgrown trees, the added shading creates an even more ominous feeling. The dark and dreary feeling created by dark colors and a lack of sunlight are enough to scare most homebuyers away. To attract more buyers, make sure your house is bright and cheery, not dark and dreary!

Lawn Condition

Have you ever driven through a neighborhood and noticed one or two lawns that are lush and green and really stand out from all the others, and then find yourself wondering what it is the homeowners are doing to make them that way? In my experience, the best way to keep your lawn looking great during the spring and summer months is by generously watering it on a regular basis, especially in warmer climates. It also helps to apply fertilizer approximately once each month to keep the grass looking green. Failure to do these two things may leave your lawn looking dry and brown. In addition to regular watering and fertilizing, the lawn should also be mowed, trimmed, and edged regularly. Don't let the grass grow too tall, and make a special effort to get the weed whacker out from time to time. Weeds that grow up along the house, around the mailbox, or anywhere else are very unsightly. It doesn't take much to keep them cut and goes a long way toward helping to maintain a pristine and neat appearance for your lawn.

One additional bit of advice is to keep a close watch for any type of lawn disease so that it can be treated immediately if any signs are detected. The type of grass in my area, along with the climate, presents conditions that are conducive to the formation of a disease known as "brown patch" or "dollar patch." When affected, the grass takes on a dead, brown appearance and spreads in a circular fashion, like a silver dollar. Knowing that this disease struck my lawn indiscriminately year after year, I chose to fight back at the first sign of any brown patches. I spent some time familiarizing myself with the products available that are used to treat the disease specifically and purchased a bottle in advance from a local home improvement store so that I would have it on hand when and if this disease struck my lawn again. Sure enough, the brown patch returned again just as it had in previous years. This time, however, I was ready for it. I treated the affected area before it got out of control and, within a few days, it was gone. For the first time in a long time, my lawn looked great. It looked so good, in fact, that my neighbors began to notice, and before long they were coming to me for advice on how to care for their lawns!

Landscaping: An Easy Way to Dress Your House for Success

As previously mentioned, pruning overgrown trees and shrubs can go a long way toward creating a more welcoming appearance, especially if they create excessive shade. One foreclosed property I recently purchased had so many shrubs and bushes growing across the front of the house that it was almost entirely obscured. Recognizing the value of creating a bright and cheery appearance, one of the first things I had my crew do was to remove them completely. Because they were so overgrown, cutting them back in this case would have left them looking butchered rather than pruned. We then dressed up the appearance of the front of the house by planting some small, inexpensive bushes and filling in the rest of the area with bark mulch.

In addition to having wildly overgrown bushes across the front of the house, there were also several trees with large branches that extended over the front and top of the house and created excessive shading. The tree branches were trimmed back to allow more sunlight and to get them away from the house to create a more open feeling. After these changes were made, the house no longer appeared dark and dreary, but was now bright and cheery! Pruning bushes, trimming trees, and dressing your house up with landscaping can go a long way toward improving its appearance. When done properly, it can also set your house apart from all the others and significantly enhance its value, as well as its marketability.

Fencing Repairs

The proper fencing around a house can make a house look welcoming, especially if it's done in good taste. For example, a white picket fence across the front of a cottage out in an open suburban area creates an aura of charm and country relaxation. On the other hand, that same fence in a worn and dilapidated condition will create a first impression that suggests the house needs a lot of work. Improvements to fencing can go a long way toward enhancing not only the appearance of your house, but the functionality of it as well. Although not all houses have fences, there are many areas in which every house in an entire neighborhood is built with a fence. This is especially true in newer communities. I've lived in areas where every house in the neighborhood had a fenced yard, and I've also lived in neighborhoods where fences weren't allowed at all, with the exception of those required by law for swimming pools.

If your house has a fenced yard and the wood is beginning to show signs of deterioration, it may be time to replace it. Replacing a fence made of cedar or a similar wood product is much more expensive than painting or power washing, so if you can get by with a fresh coat of paint or stain, I encourage you to do so. If the fence has deteriorated to the point where it is no longer usable and you can't justify the expense of replacing it, tearing it down and hauling off the debris is another inexpensive alternative. Whether you choose to remove the fence altogether or replace it will depend on what is commonly accepted in that particular neighborhood. For example, if all the surrounding houses have fences, there's a good chance yours will have to be replaced to comply with the association rules and bylaws.

A Junky Yard Can Make Your House Look Junky

Getting rid of any junk or debris that may have accumulated over the years will do wonders for any house. When a prospective buyer drives up to look at a house for sale, if years of junk and debris have accumulated in the yard, there's a good chance the buyer will keep right on driving. Creating a positive first impression is essential to presenting your home in its most favorable light, and cleaning up the junk and throwing out the trash is a great way to start.

Cleaning up trash and debris from a property is easy to do and doesn't cost very much either. If there are junky cars, old motorcycles, or engine blocks lying around, throw them out! Get rid of all of that unsightly junk! You want the outside of the property to be inviting. A lot of stuff lying around the outside is a poor reflection on the entire property and will surely create a negative first impression for a potential buyer. Sooner or later, you're going to have to get rid of the clutter, so you may as well take time to do it *before* trying to sell your house. Put yourself in the shoes of a buyer and think about how you might react to looking at a house for sale that has a bunch of junk in the front yard. Chances are you may not even bother to stop.

Following is a checklist of items to be on the lookout for in your yard. The list should by no means be considered exhaustive, but it's a good start. Allow common sense to prevail, and you'll be in good shape.

- *Bottles, cans, trash.* Clean up any old bottles and cans that may have accumulated in the yard along with general trash and debris.

Exterior Home Preparation

- *Tires.* Have you ever purchased a new set of tires, but wanted to hang onto the old ones just in case you got a flat in one of the new tires? The old tires, which were probably stacked on the side of the house or somewhere in the back yard, are probably still there to this day. Get rid of them!

- *Firewood.* Old wood cut up to be used for firewood attracts insects and is often thrown into a heap. If you're selling a house in the spring or summer, throw it out. At a minimum, stack the firewood neatly and get rid of the loose chips that may be lying around.

- *Dated playground equipment.* You may also have some playground equipment made of plastic that was bright and colorful when new, but has now become cracked and faded. Whether you throw it out, give it away, donate it to charity, or sell it in a garage sale, just get rid of it.

- *Lawn clippings and other natural waste.* You may have a spot in the back yard somewhere where the lawn clippings are dumped week after week and have now formed a small mountain, or where you throw branches broken off trees by the wind and those you have pruned. Get rid of them!

- *Bicycles and other kids' toys.* How many times have you been through a neighborhood and seen old bikes and toys strewn in front of a house? Have the kids lend a helping hand to get them put away where they belong.

Freshen Up Your House with a Fresh Coat of Paint

One of the most cost-effective ways you can improve the appearance of a house is by giving it a fresh coat of paint. If it's been more than five years since your house has seen new paint, it's probably time to apply a fresh coat. I like to think of paint as "the miracle that comes in a can" because, with each stroke of the brush, it can literally transform the appearance of a house that looks worn and dated into one that looks bright and fresh. It may also be time to update the color scheme of your house, especially if it's been more than 10 years since it has been painted. For example, while colonial blue was quite popular during the 1980s, today it would be considered dated. As a builder of new homes, virtually all of the spec houses we build have traditional brick colors like earth tones or reds, accented by light-colored earth tones like beige, linen, or taupe. Our buyers tell us these are the colors they prefer. In 10 years, we may come full circle back to colonial blue, but until we do, we're sticking with what the market demands.

Although painting a house is somewhat labor intensive, if you want to save money, it's a job that just about anyone can do. On the other hand, if you prefer not to paint or don't have the time, the work can be hired out fairly inexpensively. I suggest you take the time to shop around though, as labor prices vary widely. There was a time when I didn't think twice about grabbing a paint brush and roller and tackling a painting job myself. Now that I'm a little older, however, I don't think twice about calling a painter to hire the work out. I don't mean to suggest that I'm lazy, since that is certainly not the case. My time is better spent and more productive, however, doing other activities. Primary advantages of painting a house are that it doesn't cost very much, paint's easy to apply, and it can be done in less that a week. A fresh coat of paint can transform a house from the ugly duckling on the street to the most beautiful and graceful white swan.

Check the Condition of Siding and Repair or Replace as Necessary

Most houses have some type of siding on them. In general, older houses built 20 or more years ago likely have a siding product made from wood, while newer houses tend to be built with vinyl siding. If the house has siding made from wood or aluminum, it can easily be painted, as described in the previous section. If the siding is made of vinyl, there's a good chance it won't need to be painted at all since vinyl siding can hold its color for many years. I do recommend, however, cleaning the exterior surface by power washing it with a mild soap and bleach solution. The bleach is used to kill any mold that may be present. It's okay if you don't have a power washer because, in most areas, they can easily be rented. An alternative to power washing is to use a bucket with the cleaning solution in it and a scrub brush attached to an extension pole. While I've used both at one time or another, I don't mind using the brush method on smaller jobs, but do prefer a power washer for larger houses. Regardless of what type of siding you have, be sure it's in good condition by taking time to clean, paint, and repair as needed.

Don't Forget the Gutters and Down Spouts

I once bought a house that had a loose gutter, which had fallen off before I moved into it. The gutter had fallen to the ground and had been carelessly tossed along the side of the house. Even though I had requested that the seller repair the gutter, the day of closing came and still the gutter had not been repaired. I knew it was a simple thing to fix, so I didn't let it hold up the closing. My wife and I had just been blessed with a brand new baby boy and we were anxious to move into what would be a "new" house for us.

The day of closing had come and gone. I thought to myself that as soon as we got moved in, I would fix the gutter by reattaching it to the house. As it turned out, unpacking took longer than expected, the new baby certainly took more time than expected, and before I knew it, old man winter had come to visit for a few months. "Well, okay. I'll wait until the spring time, and then I'll fix the gutter," I thought to myself. Sure enough, spring came just as it always does, and then summer, and then fall, and before I knew it, winter had returned.

A second year passed and that gutter was still on the ground, exactly where it was when I bought the house, only now it had weeds grown up around it and was more unsightly than ever. Along came another baby boy, and two more years had passed, making four years in total, and still that gutter lay exactly where it had since the day we moved in. Before we knew it, it was time to move to another house. Knowing that creating a good first impression is vital to selling a house, I finally fixed that gutter by reattaching it to the house, which is exactly what I should have done four years ago when we moved in.

Roof Repair and Replacement

If it's been 20 or more years since the roof on your house has been replaced, it may be time for a new one, especially if there is any evidence of leaking. A leaky roof is usually fairly easy to detect by a simple inspection of the ceilings in your house. If any staining or water spots are visible on the ceiling, then there's a good chance you may have a leak. In some cases, the source of a leak can be located and patched. In other cases, if the leak is too severe and the roof is worn out anyway, then the roof will need to be replaced. Although you can sell your house "as is," if there are any problems with the roof you must fully disclose them to prospective buyers. A leaky roof that will soon need to be replaced has the potential to deter buyers. For those buyers who are interested, they will most assuredly require some type of pricing concession to be made, such as an allowance or credit at closing to cover the cost of a new roof. Many buyers don't want to fool with having the roof replaced and will quite likely pass on a house that needs extensive repairs. Unless the house is perceived to be a real bargain, buyers simply don't want to take on a major project like replacing a roof.

The cost to replace a roof can vary widely with age and condition. Most composition shingles have a minimum life of 25 years, so if the existing shingles are fewer than 15 years old, it's a pretty safe bet that any repairs required will be minimal. After 15 years, the shingles can begin to curl up and wear out to the point where leaks begin to develop. If a new roof is needed, the cost to replace it is usually not prohibitive. If, for example, a new layer of shingles can be applied over the existing layer, the cost and time involved is much less than if two or three layers of shingles already exist, which will necessitate their removal. This can effectively double the price of a new roof, as the labor required for the tear-off can be quite expensive due to the additional time required. Although no one wants to incur any more expenses than absolutely necessary, I recommend making the required investment in repairing or replacing the roof if necessary. Doing so will help the house to sell more quickly and will eliminate the possibility of concerns or objections that may otherwise be raised by a potential buyer.

Deck Condition: Restore and Refinish as Necessary

If your house has a deck or porch made of wood, be sure to check it for wear and tear, as well as for its overall appearance. Unless the deck is made from a composite like plastic or fiberglass, there's a good chance it will need to be either power washed, stained and resealed, or repainted. Most decks and porches are made of wood and are either stained or painted. While a painted finish may last up to five years, a stained finish typically lasts only one to two years. This is especially true in harsh climates.

Exterior Home Preparation

My house sits up high above the ground since it is built on what is referred to as a daylight basement. As a result, the deck sits up a full level from the ground and has two stairways uniquely designed to angle around the front and side of it. Every winter the deck takes a severe beating because it is subjected to subzero temperatures, snow, and sometimes ice. Every spring, your humble author spends one day cleaning, scrubbing, and power washing, and another day staining and finishing. I have to keep reminding myself after several hours in the sun that the process will all be worth it when I am finished. It generally takes a few days for my body to recuperate, but as I sit on the newly stained deck with my family enjoying hot dogs and hamburgers hot off the grill, I have no regrets about my preference for the beautiful, rich cedar wood.

Because decks and porches are quite popular among homeowners, cleaning and restoring the finish is very important. Cleaning and refinishing a deck can usually be done in a couple of days or less and is generally a fairly inexpensive process unless, of course, extensive repairs are needed. I recommend taking the time to repair or otherwise clean, stain, or paint your deck or porch as needed. By doing so, you will have taken one more step that will help set your house apart from the competition, thereby enabling you to achieve your objective of getting it sold!

Additional Outdoor Structures

Gazebos, sheds, and playground equipment fall into a category similar to decks and porches because they're typically made of wood. Like decks, the weather takes its toll on them. After a season or two of hot sun, driving rain, and cold winters, nature's elements will eventually diminish their appearance. In order to maximize the marketability of your house, I recommend power washing or otherwise cleaning these structures, and then painting or staining them as necessary.

Organize Your Garage to Make It Appear Larger

Most homes today have either an attached or a detached garage. I don't know about your garage, but somehow my garage seems to mysteriously fill up with "stuff." I can clean it and organize it and a month later it seems as though I've accumulated more stuff. Before I know it, the garage looks cluttered again. A garage is much like a storage shed in the sense that everyone wants a place to store their stuff. The problem is, the more space we have, the more stuff we accumulate.

I recommend that, before placing your home on the market to sell, you be sure to take the time to clean all of the junk and clutter that has accumulated over the past several years out of the garage. It's amazing how fast old and worthless stuff collects over such a seemingly short period of time. If you haven't used any of the following items in the past three or more years, it may be time to throw them out. I know that's a hard thing for many of you to do, but I have faith in you that if you really put your mind to it, you can do it. Let's take a look at some of the things that can be disposed of.

Partially full or empty containers, such as paint cans, lubricants, old jars, and bottles

Worn-out toys, such as bikes, wagons, and games

Lawn equipment in disrepair, such as mowers and yard tools

Miscellaneous items, such as empty boxes and pink flamingo yard ornaments

Once you get all of the old stuff cleaned out, the next thing to do is to organize the garage. There are a variety of inexpensive options available today for organizing and arranging a garage. Shelving that can be easily assembled and disassembled is probably the best option. That way it won't take long to put it together and you can also take it with you when you move. Another option is simply to choose to stack the items neatly in a corner. Organizing the items in your garage will not only give it a clean and uncluttered appearance, but it will also help it to appear larger. A garage full of stuff, on the other hand, makes the garage feel smaller than it actually is.

Dress Your House to Impress with a Beautiful Wooden Door

Have you ever driven through a neighborhood and seen a house that had a front door that was so spectacular it made you stop the car, or at least slow down, to get a better look at it? When I see magnificent front doors, the ones

Exterior Home Preparation

that are real showstoppers, I can't help but slow down to more fully appreciate their beauty. A beautiful front door can really accentuate the appearance of a house and helps set the tone for guests who may be visiting, as well as for those prospective buyers coming to look at your house. If your front door is made of a beautiful wood like mahogany or oak, be sure it is in showroom condition. If it needs to be refinished, I recommend spending the money to do so. If your front door is a steel insulated door, it can easily be painted and made to look like new. Be sure to inspect the hardware on the door also. If the doorknob or lock is loose or worn looking, it may be time to replace them. A beautiful entry door can create a great positive first impression of your house.

In summary, make sure your house doesn't register on the Berges Yikes-Appeal Scale. When preparing your house for resale, remember the key principle that *visibility adds value*. The more visible an improvement or repair is, the better your house will show, and the better your house shows, the easier it will be to sell. Not only that, but home improvements that fall into the "visibility adds value" category typically offer the greatest return on investment.

3

Interior Home Preparation: How to Make Low Cost, High Impact Improvements That Will Sell Your Home Fast

In the previous chapter, we focused on home improvements that
- Could easily be made to the exterior of a house
- Offered a high return for the dollars invested
- Were the most visible

Remember, before a buyer will take the time to stop and look at your house, the outside of it must be neat and clean in appearance. Buyers have to have a reason to stop and look at your house. If it looks junky on the outside, they'll reason that it must be junky on the inside. On the other hand, if your house is neat and clean on the outside, buyers will assume it must be neat and clean on the inside. In this chapter, we'll focus on those home improvements that can add the most value for the least amount of money on the inside of your house. The principle of "visibility adds value" applies just as much to the interior of a house as it does to the exterior.

Is the Inside of Your House Bright and Cheery, or Dark and Dreary?

In Chapter 2, we discussed the importance of making sure the exterior of a house does not appear dark and dreary, but rather, bright and cheery. The interior of a house is just as important, if not more so, than the exterior. Many of the houses built during the 1970s with dark brown exteriors also had dark interiors. For example, the use of brown colored paneling was quite common. I still see it today in many of the houses I look at. If the lighting is poor because of a lack of windows or existing drapes or shades, the brown paneling makes the house look all the darker. Kids' bedrooms are another prime example. While a young boy might use navy blue paint because it's the school football team's colors, not everyone wants navy blue walls. The dark paint does nothing to enhance or brighten the room. Dark colors actually do just the opposite by making the room feel smaller.

The psychological aspect of bright and cheery colors is not to be ignored either. Have you ever heard generalized comments suggesting that people living in the Northeast are not very friendly? Contrast that with comments made about people living in the South, who are supposedly friendlier. Southern climates and coastal areas have far more sunny days each year than do other regions. The amount of sunlight our bodies receive has a psychological effect on us. When the sun is out, we are happy and feel good inside. When it's overcast and gloomy, however, we long for the sun and may not feel quite as good inside. This is especially true in the winter, when there are extended periods of overcast skies. In Michigan, for example, at times it may be a whole month before the sun finally shows itself. Generally speaking, our attitudes and behavior tend to mirror the weather. If it's a beautiful day, we feel great. If it's a gloomy day, we feel lousy. To sell your house in the quickest time possible, be sure the colors in it are bright and cheery, not dark and dreary!

Clean or Cluttered?

Cleanliness and order have a significant effect on a prospective buyer's first impression of your house. As an active investor in many aspects of real estate, I've been in more houses than I can count that have been nothing less than an assault on the visual senses. I've seen dirty dishes in the sink, laundry piled high in the utility room, dog poop on the floor, old food mashed into the carpet, overfilled trashcans, toys strewn throughout the house, and the list goes on and on. These houses obviously fall into the cluttered category.

In contrast, just last week I went to look at a house that was listed for sale to preview their property. As the front door was opened, my eyes were treated to a visual feast. The interior of the home was immaculately decorated with beautiful paintings. Curio cabinets were filled with delicate figurines. Vases filled with lush, green plants were strategically placed to provide colorful accents in just the right places. Hardwood flooring, fluted molding, and ceramic tiling provided additional beauty to the home. Perhaps what impressed me the most about this particular home was that everything was neatly organized and in its place. There were no dirty dishes in the sink or old newspapers lying around, no dog poop on the floor or toys strewn about. The house made a remarkable first impression on me, and I knew it would to potential buyers as well.

If your house is not in order, spend a day or two and clean out all of the old junk lying around which you'll probably never use anyway. Besides, getting rid of the clutter now will save you from having to do it when you move. There really is a lot of truth in the old adage about "first impressions." To sell your house in the quickest time possible, be sure it creates a positive first impression by taking time to organize and clean it.

Flooring: A Low Cost, High Impact Improvement

Yikes! Is the carpet in your house bright orange or lime green with a long, shag-like appearance? If it is, then it's time to throw it out! If it's been more than five to seven years since any of the flooring in your home has been replaced, there's a good chance that it may need it now. There are a number of factors impacting the durability of flooring. For example, kids have been known to be pretty hard on flooring at times, especially if they're small children. It doesn't take long for spilled milk or juice every other day to take its toll on flooring. Pets can inflict just as much damage as children. A neighbor of mine recently told me about how his three sheep dogs (all large dogs in excess of 75 pounds) had trashed most of the rooms in his house, and, in particular, the flooring. For some reason, my neighbor laughed as he shared this with me. It seemed to me, however, that his laugh was more of a nervous laugh than a "Ha-ha, that was funny" laugh. The sheep dogs are indoor pets and are apparently free to roam as they please. Why anyone would allow an animal to completely ruin the interior of a home and thousands of dollars worth of flooring and furniture is simply beyond me. My neighbor obviously loves his dogs a great deal, but it seems to me that the line has to be drawn somewhere.

Since flooring doesn't wear out overnight, you may not have noticed the paths or walkways worn in the carpet in some of the rooms, or maybe the stains in the family room from the baby's spilled juice and milk. Oh, and are those Cheerios ground into the floor? I suggest carefully inspecting the floors in your home for some of these telltale signs of wear and tear. Moving the couch out from the wall where it has been for the last few years is a good way to determine how much wear has occurred. Compare the carpet underneath the sofa to an area where foot traffic is heavy and notice the difference. This is usually a good indicator of just how worn out it is. The bottom line is, if the carpet is old and ugly, it's time to get rid of it. Installing new flooring can do absolute wonders for most any home.

As you prepare to put your house on the market with flooring that needs to be replaced, but aren't sure whether to give the buyer a flooring allowance or replace it yourself, my advice is to spend the money now and put in the new flooring. Remember the key principle discussed in Chapter 1, *visibility adds value*. Many years ago, my wife and I put our house up for sale. The flooring in it was in fair to poor condition, and was also somewhat outdated. We decided to offer a flooring allowance to potential buyers rather than spend the money to replace it. We thought at the time that it was a perfectly rational thing to do because surely most buyers would prefer to select their own flooring. We soon discovered, however, that most buyers had a difficult time seeing the home's potential without the new flooring, even though they would be the ones picking it out. Our home was priced below market and was in good condition other than the flooring. We thought that by offering a flooring allowance, a family could move in and select its own flooring. After all, who wouldn't want to choose his or her own flooring?

As it turned out, hardly anyone wanted to. Since we had already moved into another home and didn't want to carry two payments, we ended up selling the house for about $10,000 less than what we believed its true value was. At the time, for less than half that amount, we could have replaced all of the flooring and sold the house for its full market value. There are, of course, those buyers who would prefer to choose their own flooring, but as a general rule, people like to buy a house that's ready to move into. This is especially true in more expensive neighborhoods. Many of these buyers have more money than time and much prefer to move into a house that doesn't require any fixing up. In summary, don't second-guess yourself. If the flooring is old and worn out, spend the money now and have it replaced. You're going to pay for it one way or another, so you might as well pay for it now, because doing so will help you to sell your house in the quickest time possible.

Dress Up the Inside with a Fresh Coat of Paint

I don't mean to sound like a broken record, but recall once again the principle we discussed in Chapter 1 about visibility and its relationship to value. We said that visibility adds value and the more visible an improvement is, the greater its potential to add value. This principle is especially true of painting the interior of a house, since the walls and ceiling are the most visible aspect of all. As soon as a person walks into a house, one of the very first things noticed is the color and condition of the paint. If the colors are outdated or the paint is in poor condition from years of normal wear and tear, other people entering the house will surely notice. There's a good chance you haven't noticed the poor condition of the paint in your own house, since the process of deterioration is a very gradual one. A crayon mark here and a handprint or smudge there, year after year, will eventually result in a house that desperately needs to be painted. To sell your house in the quickest time possible, I recommend making a thorough examination of the condition of the walls and ceilings and painting them as necessary.

Give Your Kitchen a Facelift

If your house is more than 15 to 20 years old and the kitchen has never been updated, it may be time to give it a makeover. Adhering to the visibility adds value philosophy, cabinets, countertops, and appliances are the most visible components of a kitchen. And in order to see these components, the kitchen must have adequate lighting. Based on feedback from the many homebuyers in our Symphony Homes' communities, cabinets are one of the most important features in a house. Consumers tell us that they like to have as much cabinet space as possible and that the cabinets should be both stylish and functional.

If you're thinking about replacing all of the cabinets in your kitchen, I suggest looking at ways to reconfigure it to maximize the number of available cabinets. I recently had all of the old cabinets removed from one of my investment properties and replaced them with a rich looking, but inexpensive, line of cherry cabinetry. I also instructed the crew to rip out the wall adjoining the family room. This had the effect of creating a more open feeling in the kitchen, which now flowed into the family room. While older houses tend to have a more choppy and sectional design, newer houses tend to be more open with one room flowing freely into the next. Another popular kitchen feature is a center island, which you may also want to consider installing if there is room to do so.

If you decide to replace the kitchen cabinets, I recommend replacing the countertops at the same time. Updating kitchen countertops is an affordable way to give your kitchen a fresh, new look while at the same time adding value to your home. Like the cabinets, if the countertops are 15 to 20 years old or more, then it's probably time to replace them. Even if you've taken good care of the countertops, and they are still in excellent condition, there's a good chance the colors and materials used when they were installed are no longer in style.

Now let's discuss another very visible component of your kitchen. Remember the once popular, but now very dated copper-tone brown, harvest gold, or avocado green colors for appliances? If you don't remember them, I'm probably dating myself, but if you still own any of these ancient relics, it's time to throw them out! I suppose if they are still in good condition, you might be able to sell them to an antique dealer, but don't get your hopes up. Even he probably won't want them. Since appliances are rather large and prominent in their appearance, it seems only natural that they would be expensive. Quite the opposite is true, however. Replacing the appliances in your kitchen is one of the easiest and least expensive home improvements you can make. Within as a little as a day or two of making your selections, you can outfit your kitchen with new appliances featuring the most current colors, styles, and features, all of which are sure to help your home sell quicker.

The best way to show off your new cabinets, countertops, and appliances is with the proper lighting. Just yesterday, I was in a young couple's house to talk to them about listing their house for sale so they could purchase one of our new homes. One of the first things I noticed was how dimly lit the kitchen was. The house, which was built in the early 1900s, was in fairly good condition, but attention to the lighting was greatly needed. The kitchen had one small light fixture above the table, and another one above the sink. Furthermore, judging by the amount of light they gave off, the fixtures couldn't have had more than 60 watt bulbs in them. In short, the kitchen was not bright and cheery, but was instead dark and dreary. An easy way to brighten any kitchen up is by replacing an existing fixture with a four-bulb fluorescent fixture. This type of light fixture is available as either a $1\frac{1}{2} \times 4$ foot or a 2×4 foot fixture and is generally priced around $100. To sell your house in the quickest time possible, I recommend replacing the cabinets and countertops, if needed, and updating the lighting to show them off!

Give Your Bathroom a Complete Makeover

Updating and modernizing bathrooms is by far one of the most popular improvements homeowners make each year. While my company's primary business is the construction of new homes, we also buy undervalued properties such as foreclosures to renovate and resell. Depending on the age and condition of the house, one of the first things we do is to rip out all of the existing cabinets, flooring, and lighting in the bathrooms. This is especially true in older houses where these items are so outdated that even antique dealers wouldn't want them. Within a couple of days, my crews give the bathroom what we refer to as the Symphony Homes complete makeover. After all of the old items are stripped out, the walls are painted, new flooring is put down, the cabinets and faucets are installed, and old rusty light strips are replaced with beautiful (but inexpensive) light fixtures. The bathrooms in these old houses are transformed from ancient and obsolete to modern and complete.

Perhaps your bathroom doesn't need a complete makeover. Maybe just applying a fresh coat of paint and replacing the lighting will do the trick. Whatever the case, I recommend *not* overlooking this very important room. To sell your house in the quickest time possible, be sure your bathroom is up to date and in good repair.

Light the Way with New Fixtures

Lighting plays a vital role in the way prospective buyers literally see a house. If there isn't enough lighting, a house can feel dark and cold. If there is too much lighting, it may create a harsh effect and even make the house feel hot, especially in warmer climates or during the summer time. The overriding philosophy of my company, Symphony Homes, is to provide customers with a quality built home backed by superb customer service at an outstanding value. One of the ways we do this is by *not* skimping on the lighting package that comes with the new homes we build. I've seen all too often brand new homes offered by other builders with the most basic of lighting packages installed in them. What many other builders fail to realize is that for just a few more dollars, they can actually purchase a nice looking, upscale lighting package for the entire home. Cheap light fixtures make the whole house look cheap. Why would someone spend $250,000 to build a house only to finish it with cheap lighting? By simply increasing their lighting budget by another $300 to $500, builders could greatly improve the way their homes show. Yes, you can spend a lot more money than $500, even for one light fixture, but you can also purchase very attractive lights for much less. To sell your house in the quickest time possible, I recommend replacing and updating the lighting in it as needed.

Clean Out Those Cluttered Closets

Although it's hard to believe that having cluttered closets could possibly make that much difference when selling a house, potential buyers will want to know where their stuff is going to go. The natural tendency for buyers walking through a house is to open practically every door in it. This includes the closet doors. If buyers see a closet that is busting at the seams, they may reconsider purchasing the house, thinking it doesn't have adequate storage space.

With just a few simple and inexpensive steps, you can create the impression that the closets in your house are roomy and organized rather than cramped and cluttered. I suggest you start by removing everything from the closets. Don't try to improve them all at once, because then your house will look like it's in a mess. Instead, start with one of the main closets that buyers are most interested in, such as the one in the master bedroom. After emptying the closet, take a close look at the condition of the paint in it. Is it bright and cheery or dark and dreary? If it's been a while since the closet has been painted, it may be due for a fresh coat. Be sure to use a light color of paint such as white, even if the bedroom is painted a different color. Brighter and lighter paint colors will help the closet to look bigger, newer, and cleaner.

If organizing your closets sounds like a lot of work, don't despair. By setting aside a few evenings, or perhaps a weekend, you can have all of them looking just like new in no time. Remember that the better your house shows, the quicker you'll be able to sell it. Keep in mind also that buyers are not just looking at *your* house. They generally have at least 10 to 15 houses on their shopping lists. Set yours apart with bright and cheery closets that are well organized and buyers are sure to take note of them.

In summary, to present the inside of your house in its most favorable light, be sure to follow the tips outlined in this chapter. Although some home improvements such as replacing the kitchen cabinets can be costly, other improvements such as applying a fresh coat of paint to the walls can

Interior Home Preparation

be relatively inexpensive, especially if you do it yourself. Most buyers don't have the time or the desire to move into a house that is in disrepair. Instead, they prefer a house that's in move-in condition. In order to sell your house in the quickest time possible, I recommend making the low cost, high impact home improvements outlined in this chapter.

4

Home Valuation: How to Price Your House to Sell for Maximum Value in Minimum Time

In this chapter, we'll discuss the importance of understanding value and why it can cost you literally thousands of dollars if you don't. We'll also learn what the difference between a comparative market analysis and an appraisal is—and how to have one done for your house free of charge. Other important topics include a discussion on the relationship between price and time, how to know whether or not to lower the price of your house, and offering terms or concessions to buyers.

Understanding the Proper Value of Your House Is Essential

I know a man who recently listed and sold his house through a friend of his who was a real estate agent. This individual purchased his house about 10 years ago for $35,000, which, at the time, he believed was a fair price. When the man initially decided to sell his house, he estimated that it had probably grown in value to $55,000 and maybe $60,000 if he was lucky. He just happened to mention this in a casual conversation to his real estate friend, who in turn told him that his house was worth much more than that. In fact, the agent told him, "List your house with me, and I'll get $140,000 for it." The man thought the agent was out if his mind and that he would never be able to sell the house for that much. The agent assured him that the market in his area had appreciated significantly in recent years because of increased housing demand.

The man agreed to let the agent sell at the recommended price, and, in less than 90 days, the agent did exactly that. He was able to sell the house for full asking price, which, remember, was more than twice what the seller thought it was worth. The seller was a homeowner and not an investor and had therefore not kept up with market prices. The real estate agent, on the other hand, was an active professional who was in tune with the market and who knew precisely which areas were hot and which areas were not. The seller's lack of knowledge almost cost him $80,000 because he didn't understand the importance of value as it applied to real estate.

The moral of this story is, "Be sure to do your homework or it could cost you literally thousands of dollars." In this example, if the man had sold the house on his own without researching property values, he would no doubt have saved himself the 6 percent commission, but it would have cost him tens of thousands of dollars in lost value from underpricing his house. I think you would agree with me that it is in your best interests to make sure you properly understand property values in your neighborhood. Failure to do so could otherwise cost you thousands of dollars.

The Comparative Market Analysis

A *comparative market analysis*, or CMA, is the method used by almost all real estate agents to estimate the worth of a house. The CMA method of estimating value is based on the premise of substitution. It maintains that a buyer would not pay any more for real property than the cost of purchasing an equally desirable substitute in its respective market. It's similar to shopping for milk at the local grocery store. If Grocer A charges

$2.00 for a gallon of milk and Grocer B charges $3.00 for the same gallon, most shoppers will choose Grocer A. This is true even if the shopper has to drive a few extra minutes to get there. At some point, however, it no longer makes sense to drive additional miles, and shoppers may relent to paying more.

The CMA method also assumes that all comparable sales used in the comparison process are legitimate arm's length transactions to help ensure accuracy of the data used in the report. A comparative market analysis furthermore provides that the comparable sales used have occurred under normal market conditions. For example, this assumption would exclude properties sold under duress, such as those of a couple going through a divorce or someone who had lost his or her job and was about to lose the home to the bank. A CMA examines several properties within a given area that have sold within the last six months or so and adjusts their value based upon similarities and differences among them. Adjustments are made for differences in amenities (such as two bathrooms versus three bathrooms), square footage, and lot size.

I strongly recommend having a comparative market analysis done on the home you are selling. Without a CMA, you will have a difficult time properly estimating the value of your house. Although you may have heard from your next-door neighbor that the neighbor down the street got a certain price for her house and, therefore, your house must be worth at least as much as hers, this is not a proper basis for value. In legal terms, this would be considered *hearsay* and therefore cannot be relied upon. To properly determine the value of a house, empirical data is needed—that is to say, hard evidence such as that found in the multiple listing service, or MLS, used by real estate agents. You need factual information that is known to be true in order to determine the value of your house.

How to Get a Free CMA

Unless you are a licensed real estate agent, you will need to find a source of access to data in the MLS. The easiest way to do this is by contacting an agent who is already familiar with home values in your neighborhood. If you have lived in your neighborhood for any length of time, you should already have a good idea of which agents are active in it. Real estate agents tend to *farm*, or focus on, specific neighborhoods. Call one who is active in your area and talk to him or her about having a CMA done for your house. Most agents will provide you with a CMA study free of charge because it gives them a way of introducing themselves and the services they offer. I suggest telling your agent the truth from the outset so that there are no hard feelings. You can say, for example, that you are leaning toward selling your own house, but that you would like to hear what he or she has to say about the services he or she can offer and, more particularly, market values in your neighborhood. This gives the agent a bona fide opportunity to sell his or her services to you, while allowing you the opportunity to better understand the value of your house. If you're honest up front with the agent, then there will be no resentment toward you. The agent is still likely to accept the appointment, knowing that in the event you are unsuccessful at selling your own house, he or she may have an opportunity to sell it at a later date.

The Appraisal Process: Why You Don't Need One–Yet

An appraisal is an estimate of an object's worth or value. Appraisals are used to determine the value of personal property as well as real property. For example, the value of jewelry can be estimated by having an appraisal done just as the value of land or houses can be determined by having an appraisal done. In *Income Property Valuation* (Boston, Massachusetts: Heath Lexington Books, 1971), author William N. Kinnard defines the appraisal process this way:

> An appraisal is a professionally derived conclusion about the present worth or value of specified rights or interests in a particular parcel of real estate under stipulated market conditions or decision standards. Moreover, it is (or should be) based on the professional judgment and skill of a trained practitioner. Its conclusions should be presented in a thoroughly logical and convincing way to a client or an interested third party who requires the value estimate to help make a decision or solve a problem involving the real estate in question.

Although an appraiser can provide you with a professional opinion of the value of your house, in my opinion, it really isn't necessary—at least not until your house is sold. Real estate agents list houses for sale every day without the aid of an appraiser. A comparative market analysis, like an appraisal, is an estimate of value. While an appraiser's estimate of value may be more thorough and comprehensive than that of an agent's derived through a CMA, it is still just an opinion of value. Some appraisers tend to render very conservative estimates, while others are a bit more aggressive.

Just a few days ago, I arranged to have an appraisal done on eight different properties that I am purchasing and will close on next week. These are new construction projects and, as a builder, I know the market in this area as well as, or better than, anyone else. The bank I am working with hired a new appraiser to render an opinion on the value of each of these properties. As it turns out, his estimate of value was low on all but one of the properties. No matter how much I tried to convince him otherwise, he was not changing his opinion. This appraiser's report will have an adverse effect on the amount of money I can borrow for each of these properties. As far as I am concerned, my opinion of the value of these properties is every bit as valid as his is, if not more so, because I have bought and sold in these areas many times. Regardless of what my opinion is, however, the bank is required to rely on the professional judgment of a licensed appraiser.

One disadvantage of hiring an appraiser is that the cost of an appraisal can range from about $250 to as much as $500, depending on the area you live in. In my experience, appraisers tend to be more conservative with their estimates of value while real estate agents may be a bit more aggressive. Regardless of who renders an opinion, remember that it is just than, an opinion. The appraisal process, while somewhat objective, is also largely subjective. That means that the estimate of value can vary depending on any number of factors. For example, if two appraisers use two different sets of houses, or comps, to render an opinion of a house, then they are almost certain to come up with two different values for the same house. In short, for the purpose of placing your house on the market for sale, a CMA is all that is needed. When your house eventually sells, however, the buyer's lender will require an appraisal for the purpose of supporting the loan amount. In most instances, because it is the buyer who is obtaining the loan, he or she will be responsible for paying for the appraisal.

Compare Your House to Others in the Area

One of the best ways to get an idea of the value of your house is to look at other houses in your area that have recently sold. For example, once you have a list of recent sales provided by a real estate agent, as contained in a CMA report, take the time to drive around your neighborhood and compare the condition and features of the other houses to yours. There is no need to go through the houses because you can generally make these assessments from the outside of the houses. The CMA report provides interior information such as the number of bedrooms and bathrooms, square footage, and various amenities. All other things being equal, if your neighbor's house is 1,500 square feet and your house is 1,600 square feet, you should be able to make an upward adjustment to the price that his sold for since your house is slightly larger. Driving through the area and looking at houses that have sold will give you the opportunity to observe the exterior condition of them. Does this house need a new roof, or has it been recently replaced? Was the house recently painted? Is it meticulously landscaped? How does it compare to your house? Look at the houses that have recently sold as if you were a buyer out shopping. You would compare and contrast their size, features, and condition to ensure you were getting the best value, just like any buyer will do when they come to look at your house.

How to Sell Your House at the Right Price for Maximum Profit

While determining the optimal price at which to sell your house depends on several factors, perhaps one of the most important things to consider is how much time you have to sell it. If you just received a job promotion and are relocating to another state, for example, you may only have three months to get your house sold before it's time to move. In this situation, I recommend setting the price of your house slightly lower than similar houses in your area so that it is competitively priced. Price is unquestionably one of the strongest motivating factors buyers consider when shopping for a house. Pricing your house below the market will help it to sell quicker.

After all, everybody likes a bargain. At the other end of the spectrum is the seller who is not in any hurry. In fact, she may be indifferent to whether or not her house sells at all. In this situation, the seller would likely price her house at the upper end of the price range for houses similar to hers. If there is something unique enough about the seller's house, she just may get her price.

Another key factor to consider when determining the optimal price for your house is its condition. Compare the condition of your house to others currently available for sale. If your house is in superior condition relative to others that are for sale, then you may very well be able to charge a premium for it. On the other hand, if your house is in need of repairs, you may want to market it as a "handyman special" and price it accordingly. Remember to price your house from the perspective of a potential buyer who will be looking at many houses. Buyers will compare and contrast all of the features and benefits offered in your house against all of those offered in other houses for sale in your area. Buyers are not necessarily looking for the best price, but rather, what they perceive the best value to be.

An important element to be aware of is that in many markets your house should be priced slightly above the actual price you would like to sell it for. For example, if after doing a CMA you determine the value of your house to be $145,000, I recommend pricing it slightly above that at, let's say, $147,900, or maybe even $149,900. In general, you may receive an offer anywhere from 0 to 5 percent lower than the asking price. Everyone likes to feel like they are getting a deal, so quite often they will offer less than full price. If a buyer offers less than full price on a house listed at $147,900, you should still end up with a price that is close to your true objective, which in this example is $145,000. This strategy will vary depending on the strength of the market you are in. If the market is strong and houses are selling quickly, you can probably get away with pricing it at market. Buyers know they had better offer close to full price in a strong market because if they don't, somebody else will be right behind them who will.

Know Your Bottom Line Before You Begin to Sell

After setting the price at which you will offer your house for sale, you should be prepared in advance to have a minimum price you are willing to accept.

Home Valuation

Depending on how long your house is on the market for sale, that number may change. For example, if you recently began offering your house for sale, you may not be as flexible on what you are willing to accept. On the other hand, if you've been trying to sell your house for several months, you may be willing to accept a little less. If you've priced your house appropriately to begin with, the minimum price you are willing to accept should not be that much less than the offering price. While you should keep in mind the pricing strategy discussed in the previous section—offering your house for sale slightly above your true objective—you should also be mentally prepared to accept less.

Terms and Seller Concessions

In addition to having a predetermined minimum price you are willing to accept, you should also know whether or not you are willing to offer any type of owner financing or seller concessions the buyer may ask for. For example, if a buyer can't come up with the full down payment, it may be helpful if the seller is willing to provide financing directly to the buyer. When seller financing, or owner financing as it is also known, is used, the buyer makes payments directly to the seller under whatever terms and conditions the two parties agree on. The seller, whose interest is secured in the form of a second mortgage, receives payments from the buyer over a period of time that is agreed upon by both parties. The note may be paid over a period of 5, 10, or even 15 years. It may also include a balloon payment in which the note would be due in its entirety in 3 years. Notes can be structured in any number of ways to meet the needs of both the buyer and the seller. As the seller, you may prefer not to offer any type of financing to the buyer for whatever reason.

In addition to owner financing, buyers sometimes ask for seller concessions. Seller concessions include things like having the seller contribute a certain dollar amount or percentage of the sales price to the closing costs. Just last week, for example, I received an offer on one of our new houses that included a 3 percent seller concession. The house was listed for sale at a price of $175,000. This means the buyer was asking me to contribute $5,250 toward his closing costs. I countered his offer by agreeing to contribute a fixed dollar amount of $3,500. In addition, I raised his offering price by $3,000 to help offset the amount he was asking me to contribute. As it turned out, the buyer was already at his maximum borrowing power and therefore at his upper limit, so he ended up rejecting my counteroffer. In summary, you should be prepared in advance to know whether or not you are willing to offer any type of owner financing or seller concessions that the buyer may ask for.

Average Days on Market

The length of time it will take to sell your house will depend on a variety of factors, the first of which is the strength of the market in your area. If the market is fairly strong, your house could sell in as little as a few days. On the other hand, if the market is fairly weak, it could take a year or more to sell your house. Perhaps the best way to determine the strength of your market is to look for a term on the CMA report that is referred to as *days on market*, or DOM. On the individual comparable sales reports, the listing date along with the selling date is provided, from which DOM is calculated. DOM is simply the sales date minus the listing date. The number is used by real estate agents to help gauge the strength of neighborhoods, and even entire cities or towns. A DOM of 25, for example, means that from the time the house was placed on the market for sale until the time an offer was accepted on it was 25 days. This is very useful information to sellers because it provides a general indication of how long it will take to sell their houses.

Additional factors that will determine how long it will take to sell your house are its price and condition. If your house is priced appropriately relative to the market, then it should fall in line with the average days on market by other houses in the area. If the house is priced below market, then, as a general rule, it should sell more quickly than the average DOM. Conversely, if the house is priced above market, then it will likely take longer than the average DOM. The condition of your house relative to the condition of other houses in your area will also affect the length of time it takes to sell it. If your house is in excellent condition, shows very well, and is appropriately priced, then it should sell faster than the average DOM. And conversely, if your house is in poor condition and priced the same as a house in better condition, then it will likely take longer than the average DOM.

Time Is Money

If your house has been on the market longer than 90 to 120 days, it may be time to consider lowering the price. While the decision of whether or not to lower the price is dependent on several factors, the most important of these is your timing and sense of urgency. If you are in no hurry to sell and it really doesn't matter one way or another whether you stay in your house or move, then you may consider leaving the price where it is for as long as 180 days, or even longer if you want to. On the other hand, if you are relocating to another area or have already purchased another house, then you should consider lowering the price. The proverbial wisdom that *time is money* especially holds true in this instance because every day your house isn't sold literally costs you money. Unless you own your house free and clear, the interest clock doesn't stop ticking just because you have to move or you have already purchased another home. In short, the decision to lower the price on your house is largely dependent upon other commitments you have already made or those you anticipate making. These commitments affect how motivated you are and largely determine your sense of urgency.

In summary, to sell your house at the right price and for maximum profit, you'll need to have a comparative market analysis done on your house. Although a CMA is essential to setting the price of your house correctly, a formal appraisal is not. Remember also to be aware of the average number of days on market it takes houses in your area to sell and set your price accordingly. If the market is fairly strong in your area or you are in no hurry to sell, then it's safe to set the price of your house at the upper end of the price range. On the other hand, if the market is moderate to weak in your area or you need to sell quickly, then you should adjust the price of your house accordingly.

5

Third-Party Reports and Legal Forms: How to Protect Yourself by Using These Essential Forms

One of the most important aspects of selling a house is to make sure it is done with the proper legal documents. From drafting a purchase agreement to providing disclosures, legal forms are essential to completing the sale of your house. It's safe to assume that the majority of readers of this book are not attorneys and would therefore welcome the assistance provided herein to better understand the various legal documents used when selling a house. In this chapter, we'll begin by discussing whether or not you need to hire an attorney to represent you when selling your house, and then take an in-depth look at 10 essential real estate forms that are commonly used by FSBOs.

Professional Legal Services

Using an attorney to help close the sale of your house is completely optional. To my knowledge, there are no laws in any state that require you to hire an attorney to review the closing documents. There are lenders, however, that may require borrowers to pay for certain attorney services that are required to prepare loan documents. While this is often true for larger transactions, it is not always the case. For example, tomorrow morning, I am closing on eight separate loans totaling $1.5 million with one of the lenders I work with. This particular lender prepares all of the closing documents internally so there are no attorney fees. In contrast, I am closing nine separate loans totaling $1.9 million at the end of this month with another lender. This particular lender uses an attorney to prepare all of the closing documents. The fees from the attorney are passed through to the client, which in this case is me. According to the lender, the fees are estimated to be about $3,000, a figure I'm not overly excited about having to pay. I recommend asking your lender or mortgage company what their policy is regarding attorney fees.

Although your lender may or may not require the use of an attorney, you may still want to consider using one, especially if you are not familiar with real estate documents. A sales contract may have language in it, for example, that is written to protect the buyer's interests rather than the seller's. In most states, there are many aspects of the sales contract that are negotiable. This includes closing costs. Closing costs are usually shared by both the buyer and the seller, but they don't always have to be. Some states require that certain costs be paid by either the buyer or the seller, unless otherwise specified. For example, in Michigan the seller is required to pay what is known as a *state transfer tax*, unless otherwise expressly stipulated in the agreement. A transfer tax is essentially the same thing as a sales tax that is placed on consumer goods, only it is a tax on the sale of land, houses, or any other type of real estate. If you don't know the law in your area and fail to review the contract carefully, you could end up contractually obligating yourself to terms that are not in your best interests. On the other hand, if you have bought and sold real estate before and are familiar with contract law, then you can probably get by without using an attorney.

I personally rarely use an attorney when buying and selling real estate. My experience with attorneys is that they often tend to justify the fees they charge by making a fuss over minor and seemingly insignificant points. I placed a 70-acre residential development project that was in foreclosure by the owner under contract last month. Although the seller was ready to accept my offer, the attorney representing him kept delaying acceptance of the offer by countering on fine points of the law. After two weeks of wrangling with the agent representing the seller, I finally got fed up and gave him an ultimatum. I called the agent first thing in the morning and told him, "Barry, I'm tired of waiting for your client to accept my offer. His attorney is holding this deal up. Your client either wants to sell his property to me or he doesn't. Tell him that he has until 5:00 today to accept my offer or I will withdraw it and will expect my earnest money deposit to be returned to me in full." Hearing the seriousness in my voice, Barry immediately called his client and conveyed my growing impatience to him. By 3:00 that afternoon, the seller had accepted my offer and I had a fully executed option to purchase agreement for his property on my desk. I don't always use this kind of tactic with parties I do business with, but in this particular instance, I had grown weary of dickering with the seller's attorney over the finer points of law. The seller and his attorney needed a push to get them off the fence. I merely obliged them.

Ten Essential Real Estate Forms

Whether you are buying or selling property, real estate contracts and forms will be needed to expressly stipulate what both parties are agreeing to. Ten of the more common forms are listed below. Although you won't need all of these forms on any one transaction, it's a good idea to be familiar with them and to have them on hand just in cast you do. Samples of each of these forms are included in Appendix C.

1. Residential Sales Contract
2. Property Condition Disclosure
3. Lead-Based Paint Disclosure
4. Third-Party Financing Addendum
5. Loan Assumption Addendum

6. Seller Financing Addendum
7. Promissory Note
8. Notice of Termination
9. Warranty Deed
10. Quit Claim Deed

Real Estate Form 1: Residential Sales Contract

The residential sales contract, or purchase agreement as it is also known, is used to legally bind two or more parties together in a contractual relationship so as to specify the terms and conditions under which real property is to be bought or sold. Sales contracts are written with many different modifications to cover the various needs of the parties involved. A residential sales contract can be as short as one page, or as long as 15 or more pages. Some are written with simplicity in mind, while others are more carefully drafted for the purpose of protecting buyers and sellers from most any unforeseen condition that may arise. Regardless of their length or complexity, most all sales agreements have several primary components in common. Basic items to be covered in a purchase agreement should include at a minimum the following elements:

- Contract date
- Purchaser and seller to be identified
- Subject property street address and legal address
- Sales price
- Financing considerations
- Closing and possession dates
- Title insurance provisions
- Earnest money deposit
- Proration of any taxes due, as well as homeowner's associates dues, utility bills, or other fees
- Right of purchaser to inspect, waive rights, or accept the property "as is"
- Any additional provisions that the buyer and seller may agree to not covered in the standard agreement

Of the 10 forms described in this chapter, the residential sales contract is the most important because it is used every time real property is bought and sold. Most other real estate forms are supplementary in nature. An entire chapter has been devoted to the residential sales contract to help you more fully understand this important document. Refer to Chapter 10 for a complete discussion of the residential sales contract.

Real Estate Form 2: Property Condition Disclosure

The Seller's Disclosure of Property Condition form is intended to have the seller fully disclose to the buyer any and all property defects or conditions that warrant repair. At one time, the Latin term *caveat emptor* was used as the prevailing rule. The term means *let the buyer beware*. In other words, it was up to the buyer to use the process of discovery to detect any repair the property may have been in need of, and the seller had little to no obligation to disclose anything. The courts have in recent years begun to lean more toward protecting the buyer and placing a much greater burden on the seller than they have in the past. The prevailing law now requires sellers to disclose known property defects to the buyer. Depending on what is wrong with the property, the seller may claim that she was unaware of a particular condition that the buyer discovered after closing and taking possession. In a situation like this, the buyer must be able to present compelling evidence that the seller was in fact aware that the defect existed.

The Seller's Disclosure of Property Condition is presented in five sections and requires the seller to make the information available to the buyer after filling out the form in its entirety. Section 1 of the form contains a checklist of items such as appliances, HVAC equipment, pools, fences, and other items that are to be included with the sale of the house. The seller is required to address each item on the form by writing yes, no, or unknown in the appropriate blank. It also asks the seller to disclose any known defects in the items listed in this section. Section 2 addresses structural items such as walls, roofs, foundations, and windows, and again asks the seller to disclose known defects with any of these components. Section 3 asks the seller to provide information regarding damage from termite infestation, water damage, toxic waste, radon gas, or other such conditions. Section 4 asks the seller once again to disclose any item that is in need of repair. Finally, Section 5 addresses the seller's awareness of known modifications to the house or any of its structural components such as room additions. It also asks the seller to provide information regarding homeowner's association fees, maintenance fees, or lawsuits that may be pending against the seller that may adversely affect the sale of the property.

The safest way to protect yourself as the seller is to be honest and disclose all known defects to the buyer up front. If you have accurately and honestly filled out the Seller's Disclosure Form to the best of your ability, and the buyer has received and signed a copy of it, then you should have nothing to worry about from the standpoint of being sued at some future date. The purchaser's signature on the disclosure form is a legal acknowledgment of his or her awareness and acceptance of the property's condition at the time of sale. Furthermore, buyers have the opportunity to order a home inspection by a certified inspector if they choose. If this right is waived at the time the purchase agreement is completed, and the buyer accepts the property "as is," then he or she also waives all rights to future litigation. Think about it. If you have openly disclosed all known defects and the buyer has waived the right of inspection and has furthermore agreed in writing that he or she is willing to accept the property in its current condition, then there is no legal ground for him or her to stand on in the event a defect is discovered after the sale. The Seller's Disclosure of Property Condition is an absolutely essential form that must accompany the sale of single-family residential property. Complete this form as accurately and honestly as you can; be sure the buyer has signed and received a copy of it; and you should have nothing to worry about!

Real Estate Form 3: Lead-Based Paint Disclosure

The known presence of lead-based paint *must* be disclosed for all houses, especially those built prior to 1978. The paint that was used in houses built in 1978 or before often contained lead, a substance known to pose certain health risks that result from lead poisoning. The Environmental Protection Agency, or EPA, has issued the following statement pertaining to lead-based paint.

> Every purchaser of any interest in residential real property on which a residential dwelling was built prior to 1978 is notified that such property might present

exposure to lead from lead-based paint that may place young children at risk of developing lead poisoning. Lead poisoning in young children may produce permanent neurological damage, including learning disabilities, reduced intelligence quotient, behavioral problems, and impaired memory. Lead poisoning also poses a particular risk to pregnant women. The seller of any interest in residential real property is required to provide the buyer with any information on lead-based paint hazards. A risk assessment or inspection for possible lead-based paint hazards is recommended prior to purchase.

If your house was built prior to 1978 and you have no knowledge of lead-based paint having been used, there is a place on the form for that. By checking this box, you are not stating that lead-based paint wasn't used, but rather that you have no knowledge of lead-based paint being used. By the same token, if you are aware of and do have knowledge of lead-based paint being used at one time or another, federal law requires that you disclose this fact.

Real Estate Form 4: Third-Party Financing Addendum

The Third-Party Financing Condition Addendum requires that "a buyer shall apply promptly for all financing described…and make every reasonable effort to obtain financing approval." The addendum provides a greater level of detail for buyers seeking such third party financing as a bank loan or mortgage than does the sales contract. The addendum furthermore has provisions for buyers seeking a conventional loan, veteran's housing assistance, FHA financing, or a VA guaranteed loan. Finally, the form sets forth the terms and conditions required by the buyer to meet his or her financing needs should a third party loan be desired. While this form may or may not be required to sell your house, you should nevertheless be familiar with it in the event additional detail is required for financing provisions.

Real Estate Form 5: Loan Assumption Addendum

The Loan Assumption Addendum provides a greater level of detail to those buyers who may desire to assume a loan held by the seller. The form includes provisions for verification of the buyer's creditworthiness by requesting such information from the buyer as a credit report, verification of employment, and verification of funds available for the down payment. Although this particular addendum grants sole discretion to the seller to determine the buyer's creditworthiness, more often than not it is the mortgage company that has sole discretion. Most lenders incorporate into their mortgage documents a due-on-sale clause that may preclude the transfer of title through a loan assumption. Years ago, when interest rates were much more stable, loan assumptions were very common and due-on-sale clauses were rarely seen. Today, however, while the ability to assume a loan still exists, it generally requires the lender's review and approval of the new borrower. Moreover, the lender typically charges an origination fee just as if it were a new loan. Often, lenders have the right to adjust the interest rate at their sole discretion if the loan is assumed, so it may be just as easy for your buyer to get a new loan as it is to assume an existing one. While there's a good chance your existing loan may not be assumable, you should nevertheless be aware that such a form exists and is available to facilitate the transfer of the note from one owner to the next.

Real Estate Form 6: Seller Financing Addendum

A homeowner's willingness to provide seller financing is one of the best ways I know to get a house sold. In many instances, buyers do not have adequate savings to purchase a house and, without the aid of a seller, they would be unable to do so. For those readers who may not be familiar with the way seller financing works, allow me to share an example with you. I recently sold an investment property of mine for $65,000 to a woman who was a first-time homeowner. Because she had a low credit rating, she was only able to qualify for a 90 percent loan, which in this case amounted to $58,500. The lender would allow a seller carry back for the remaining 10 percent, or $6,500. A *seller carry back* is the same thing as seller financing. I agreed to carry the note at a rate of 12 percent interest for a period of one year, after which time she would attempt to refinance the property at 100 percent so that she could repay me. While you may think a rate of 12 percent is a bit on the high side, perhaps even usurious, I charge what the market will bear. In this situation, the woman purchasing my house had lousy credit. My willingness to provide her with seller financing allowed this lifetime apartment renter to participate in the American dream by becoming a homeowner. After only one year, she can refinance and get a more favorable rate.

The Seller Financing Addendum is similar to the other financing addenda in that it demands sufficient credit documentation to be furnished by the buyer. The primary difference here, however, is that since the seller is the one providing the financing, he or she will have sole discretion of determining the creditworthiness of the buyer. This addendum also contains a provision enabling the parties to outline the terms and conditions of the promissory note that will be created for the seller financing. The note provides for a choice of either a single payment, also known as a *balloon payment*; a standard note amortized over a predetermined period of time; or an initially interest-only note that then changes to an interest-plus-principal note that continues until the note is repaid in full. Although the repayment arrangements in this promissory note section offer buyers and sellers a limited number of ways to structure debt payments, they are some of the more common methods preferred. The repayment of debt can be structured in whatever ways the parties choose to agree upon and are by no means limited to the methods illustrated here.

In the next section of this form, it is the Seller Financing Addendum that provides for the deed of trust or mortgage that is used to secure the note. The Seller Financing Addendum may furthermore grant the right to the buyer to sell the property without prior consent of the seller, or it may instead require consent. As the seller carrying the note, I recommend adding a provision similar to a due-on-sale clause that would preclude the buyer from selling the property without first paying off the underlying obligation to the seller. This gives the buyer the flexibility he or she is seeking for the purchase of your house, while leaving you in control. Like the bank, you can either grant or deny the assumption of the note to another buyer. If the provision is included, as the seller you will then have the option of being cashed out if the property is sold before the note to you has been fully repaid.

Finally, the Seller Financing Addendum contains a provision for escrow payments for taxes and insurance that may or may not be required by you as the seller. If you are only carrying a small note, say less than 10 percent, then in all likelihood you will not set up an escrow account. I do recommend, however, that proof of annual or semiannual tax and insurance payments be provided to you as evidence that the payments have been made and do not become delinquent. If, on the other hand, you are carrying the entire note and there is no other lender involved, you will more than likely want to set up an escrow account so that the taxes and insurance can be paid when they become due.

Real Estate Form 7: Promissory Note

Unless you provide the buyer with seller financing, you will not need a promissory note. The promissory note is a document used to outline the terms and conditions under which a lender has agreed to loan money. Whether the lender is a mortgage company, a bank, or the homeowner makes no difference. All three will require that a promissory note be fully executed. Notes may be either secured or unsecured. If the note is secured, that means there is some type of physical asset being held as collateral. Most of the time, the collateral given is the property or item that the note is made against. In the case of real estate, the collateral is most likely to be the property for which the note is being made. However, it doesn't have to be. It could be anything else the borrower has that may be of some worth or value to the seller. It could be a boat; it could be a car; or it could be a vacant lot or other real property. If the note is unsecured, that means there is no collateral being used to secure the note. The seller or lender is accepting on good faith that the borrower will have the ability to repay the loan. Usually that good faith is supported by the borrower's proven credit history, which has demonstrated in the past the ability to repay a loan or other financial obligation.

The promissory note also contains provisions for the repayment terms stipulated in the note. These include the amount of the loan, the interest rate and amortization or repayment period, and any prepayment penalties that may be imposed for paying off the note prematurely. In addition, the note may contain an acceleration clause which would necessitate the note's being repaid immediately should certain conditions, such as the transfer of ownership to another party, arise. Finally, other lender requirements that may also be included in a promissory note are escrow provisions for taxes and insurance, minimum insurance amounts, the standard of care for property condition, a due-on-sale clause, and default provisions.

Real Estate Form 8: Notice of Termination

The Notice of Termination Contract is one form that, hopefully, you will not need. The form is self-explanatory in that it provides the buyer with the means to cancel or terminate the sales contract. The Notice of Termination does not grant buyers the right to terminate without just cause. The buyer can only terminate for legitimate reasons as set forth in the sales agreement, such as not being able to qualify for financing. While you probably will not need this form to sell your house, it is a good idea to be aware of it in the event that your buyer terminates his or her agreement with you.

Real Estate Form 9: Warranty Deed

Depending on where your actual closing is held, you may or may not need a deed. That isn't to say that a deed won't be needed, because it surely will. If the closing is held at a title company's or attorney's office, however, those individuals will be responsible for preparing the deed and you, therefore, will not need to. It is nevertheless important to understand the function and purpose of deeds. A *warranty deed* is the most commonly used type of deed. It is a formal written instrument by which title to real property is transferred from one owner to another and is used specifically to guarantee that the title is free and clear of any and all encumbrances. There are two parties to a deed—the grantor and the grantee. The grantor is the seller and the grantee is the purchaser.

Every deed should contain an accurate description of the property being conveyed. It should be signed and witnessed according to the laws of the state where the property is located and it should be *delivered* to the purchaser on the day of closing. I emphasize the word delivered because, until the deed is actually given, or delivered, to the buyer, there is no transfer of title. While this may sound like a rather insignificant point, it is in fact a very important one. I mention this because I am currently dealing with tax issues in two different communities I own, both related to this very principle. A few years ago I placed all of the remaining lots in both communities under contract with an option agreement. In both instances, deeds were created and placed in escrow to secure my position. I had what is referred to as an *equitable* interest in these lots. All of the deeds were dated according to the date of the option agreements. When

I finally did exercise my right to purchase the lots under the option agreements, the deeds that had been in escrow for several years were then delivered to me. Unfortunately, the deeds were all dated the same date as the option agreement. When these records were submitted to the county for recording, it appeared as though I had owned the lots for several years. This event then triggered an uncapping of the assessed values of the property extending back to the dates that were on them. This in turn triggered a series of tax increases. The county tax assessor's office has since notified me that unless I pay these so-called back taxes, they will place a tax lien against the lots. My attorney has since drafted a letter to the county officials that rests upon the notion of delivery, stating that because the deeds had not been delivered, no transfer occurred. We will continue to work together to get these rather taxing issues resolved (no pun intended).

Real Estate Form 10: Quit Claim Deed

A *quit claim deed* is used to transfer whatever interest the maker of the deed may have in a particular parcel of land. A quit claim deed is often given to clear the title when the grantor's interest in a property is questionable. Unlike a warranty deed, which guarantees clear title, a quit claim deed offers no such protection. By accepting a quit claim deed the buyer assumes all the risks. Such a deed makes no warranties as to the title, but simply transfers to the buyer whatever interest the grantor has. Quit claim deeds are used for special circumstances in which the deed needs to be transferred from one person to another, or one entity to another. For example, if a loved one's parent dies and there is a provision in the will stating the son or daughter is to inherit the property, a quit claim deed can be used to transfer title. As an active real estate investor, I own and operate several different limited liability corporations, or LLCs. I recently used a quit claim deed to transfer my interest from one legal entity to another because it was inadvertently placed in the wrong LLC when I purchased it. Although, in most FSBO situations, a warranty deed is used rather than a quit claim deed, it is nevertheless a good idea to be familiar with it and how it can help in certain conditions.

To summarize, whether you are buying or selling property, real estate contracts are an essential part of every transaction and are needed to expressly stipulate what both the buyer and the seller are agreeing to. In this chapter we discussed 10 of the more common forms used when selling property. Although you won't need all of these forms for any single transaction, it's a good idea to be familiar with them and to have them available just in case. Samples of each of the forms discussed in this chapter are included in Appendix C.

PART II

The FSBO's Marketing and Sales Checklist

6

Strategic Marketing: Seven Smart Ways to Sell Your House

To sell your house in the quickest time possible, I recommend doing everything you can to increase its exposure. The more people who know that your house is for sale, the greater your chances are for getting it sold. By making your house available to as many potential buyers as possible, you are increasing the probability that it will sell quickly and at a price that represents full market value. According to a study conducted in 2003 by the National Association of Realtors, or NAR, titled *Profile of Home Buyers and Sellers*, primary information sources used by prospective homebuyers to find a house included

- Real estate agent: 86%
- Yard sign: 69%
- Internet: 65%
- Newspaper: 49%
- Home book/magazine: 35%
- Open house: 48%
- Builders: 37%

- Television: 22%
- Relocation company: 14%

While the study cited by the NAR is helpful, not all of the methods apply to the FSBO. Real estate agents, for example, would not apply, and the individual selling only one house couldn't justify the budget to implement a full-blown television marketing campaign. Builders and relocation companies aren't applicable to the FSBO either. On the other hand, newspapers, real estate publications, the Internet, yard signs, and open houses are all excellent methods of marketing your house, and, according to the study, are sources actually used by individuals searching for a house to purchase. Other methods not cited in the study include spreading the word by networking in various professional, personal, or social affiliations, and distributing flyers throughout your community and anywhere else you think may be appropriate. When combined together, these seven methods of marketing can help bring more buyers to you than you know what to do with, thereby enabling you to sell your house for the best possible price!

Prepare a Generous Marketing Budget to Sell Your House

One of the drawbacks of selling your house on your own is that it will cost money to do so and thereby reduce the savings derived from not paying a commission. When you list your house with a real estate agent, the agent is, of course, responsible for incurring those costs. If the agent doesn't sell your house for whatever reason, you're not out anything because it is the agent who has incurred the cost of marketing your property and not you. By assuming responsibility for selling your own house, you also assume responsibility for the marketing budget. You should be prepared to spend anywhere from $50 to $250 per week on average. This figure will depend on how aggressive you intend to be with your marketing efforts, as well as on advertising costs for newspaper and real estate publications in your particular area. Rates are typically determined by readership and circulation. The more readers the newspaper has, the more papers they print, and the more papers they print, the more value they offer to advertisers. It's all about the level of

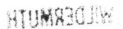

Table 6.1 Advertising Budget

Advertising Medium	Weekly Rate	Number of Weeks	Total Budget
Local Newspaper	$35	12	$420
Metropolitan Newspaper	$75	12	$900
Real Estate Magazine	$50	12	$600
Signs	$50	1	$50
Flyers	$10	12	$120
Fuel	$5	12	$60
Total	$225	12	$2,150

exposure the papers provide. Larger metropolitan papers have a much higher circulation than do smaller local papers. Consequently, the rates they charge tend to be higher. In addition to printed advertising, you'll have expenditures for signs, flyers, and any additional fuel costs you may have from running around.

Table 6.1 illustrates a general outline of some of the marketing and advertising expenditures you should be prepared for. The variables in the table are the advertising mediums you choose, the rate they charge, and the number of weeks it takes to sell your house. Depending on how strong the housing market is in your area, I recommend planning for a minimum of 12 weeks. By the time you get the word out and begin showing your house, it could quite easily take 12 weeks to get it sold. Now take a moment to review Table 6.1.

How to Use Newspapers and Classified Ads to Sell Your House

Placing ads in the local newspaper is one of the more common methods of marketing your house. One limitation of classified ads is that, depending on the newspaper, the readership may be limited to the immediate area. Bigger papers such as those found in large metropolitan areas provide greater exposure, but since there are more ads in the real estate for sale section, it makes it more difficult for your ad to stand out. You can

WILDERMUTH

compensate for this drawback by paying a little extra to highlight the heading of your ad in bold. Many newspapers also provide special sections where sellers can run a small display ad relatively inexpensively. I'm sure you're familiar with the old adage, "A picture is worth a thousand words." That is especially true in real estate. Figure 6.1 is an example of a small display ad. The picture helps paint an image in the reader's mind while providing the reader with some basic information about the house.

It's also a good idea to attempt to determine where the buyers in your area are likely to come from. For example, while many of the new homes my company builds are located in Genesee County, a lot of our buyers come from North Oakland County, which lies just south of Genesee

Figure 6.1

A BREATHTAKING

Work of Art!

Featuring
The Arietta 1750 sq ft
3 bdrm, 2 1/2 bath, 2 car garage!
Chef's kitchen with center island!
Magnificent 2 story great room!
Hardwood floors, elegant entry!
Dramatic fireplace, many extras!

ONLY $229,900!

(810) 658-3600
www.symphony-homes.com

County. This is because they can get a lot more house for the money in Genesee County than they can in North Oakland County. A proper understanding of these market trends is invaluable to us and, as a result, a large portion of our advertising budget is devoted to the North Oakland County area. If you are aware of similar market dynamics in your area, then it's a good idea to focus your advertising dollars in those publications that will best allow you to capitalize on them.

Keep Your Ads Crisp and Concise

I suggest listing only such essentials in a classified ad as the location, number of bedrooms, price, and a telephone number to call. The ad should be written in a crisp and concise format without being too wordy. Using a little bit of descriptive language is okay, just be careful not to overdo it. The idea is to whet the reader's appetite by giving him or her just enough information to pique the curiosity. I recommend including the price because doing so weeds out a lot of buyers who may not be qualified or who may be qualified but want a more expensive house. If readers see the price and know they can't afford it, they won't waste their time, or yours, by calling and asking a lot of questions. The idea is to prequalify the buyer so that you aren't getting a lot of phone calls from people who can't afford your house. The example shown as Figure 6.2 uses a reverse print to help the ad stand out from among all the other hundreds that yours will be competing with. Instead of using the standard black lettering on a white background, the ad is written with white lettering on a black background. Note also how the ad is designed to appeal to the reader's emotions by painting a visual picture for them. The ad beckons the reader to pick up the telephone and call for more information on this seemingly once in a lifetime opportunity.

Figure 6.2

Lake Orion Waterfront Property! Enjoy over 2400 sq ft in this 4-2-2 with sunset view of all sports lake! Cedar deck, large yard, and private dock complete this beautiful 2 story house! Priced to see at only $449,900! Call (555) 123-4567!

How to Use Real Estate Magazines to Sell Your House

Local real estate magazines are also a terrific way to market your house. These magazines are generally placed near grocery stores, hair salons, real estate offices, and gas stations and are made available to the public free of charge. The advertising rates are often comparable to that of a classified ad in the newspaper. These publications differ from classified ads in that they have a lot more display ads in which you can include more information about your property, as well as a photo. Also, unlike classified ads, which have hundreds of categories (cars for sale, help wanted, etc.), real estate magazines focus solely on those services related to the real estate industry. Furthermore, people who pick up the magazines are more likely to be interested in buying a house because they know what type of information is contained in them—that is, houses available for sale. There are also magazines that cater specifically to the FSBO market that are becoming increasingly available in most larger metropolitan areas. Moreover, many of these magazines offer a free listing on their related Web site when you advertise in the magazine. The FSBO magazine is especially appealing to buyers looking to save money on the purchase of a home because of the underlying notion that these homes are competitively priced because of the savings from commissions.

How to Use the Internet to Market and Sell Your House

Another way of marketing your house is by making it available for all the world to see on a Web site. Don't underestimate the power of the Internet. It can attract prospective buyers from all across the country, and, for that matter, from all across the globe. According to the study referred to at the beginning of this chapter that was conducted by National Association of Realtors, fully 65 percent of all people searching for a house used the Internet as an information source. That means that two out of every three buyers use the Internet in one way or another when searching for a house to buy, a figure that should not be ignored. I can personally attest that the Internet is by far one of the biggest lead generators for my company, Symphony Homes. The primary Web site address is www.symphony-homes.com. There is a place on the site available to people who want additional information. By filling out the form and clicking on the submit button, an e-mail is sent to us automatically, which we can then respond to. Our Web site is designed to be a source of information that prospective buyers can use to learn about our company. I must stress that it is only a starting point. We strive to create a positive first impression for buyers who will, after spending time on our site, call one of our model home centers or request additional information. The sales agents are then able to work with the buyers to answer additional questions. The Symphony Homes Web site provides us by far with the best advertising bang for the buck. We've sold new homes to buyers who found us on the Internet from as far away as Germany and Australia to as close as just across town.

There are a number of sites that cater to FSBOs by allowing them to make their houses available for sale directly on the site. As mentioned in the previous section, many of the FSBO magazines will offer advertisers free listings on their Web sites. A large number of the more traditional real estate publications that cater to all sellers also offer listings on their Web sites. While many publications offer Internet listings free of charge, others charge a nominal fee for this service. If you have trouble finding a service that caters specifically to the FSBO in your area, you can do a search on one of the major search engines like Google or Yahoo to locate one. Another good Internet source that increases your house's marketing exposure is the local newspaper, as we've already discussed. Almost all major newspapers now list their entire classified section on Web sites. This information is generally kept very current as the Web sites are updated either daily or weekly, depending on how often the paper is published.

How to Use a Yard Sign to Sell Your House

Citing the NAR study once again, 69 percent of buyers responding to the survey stated that yard signs were used as a source of information in their search for a home. Signs come in all shapes and sizes. The most commonly used size is either 18 inches by 24 inches or 24 inches by 30 inches. Either one of these sizes is fine. Signs any smaller than this are difficult to see. I recommend having a sign that is professionally made instead of one of the less expensive types found in hardware stores. A professionally made sign is inviting to buyers and helps create a strong first impression. Many FSBO Internet sites sell signs, so you shouldn't have any problem finding one. In addition, some hardware stores sell the larger size along with the steel frame they fit in. Vinyl lettering or numbering can be used to customize your message. You may even want to consider placing two signs in your yard, depending on its size and configuration. For example, if you live on a corner, you may want to place a sign on each side of the house so that drivers traveling on either of the two roads can see it. Smaller directional signs are also a good idea, especially if your house is not located near the front of your community or a comparable high traffic location.

Information Boxes Are for Everyone (Including Your Nosy Neighbors)

There are two schools of thought on having an information box attached to the yard sign. The first is that it's a great place to make flyers immediately available to potential buyers who may be interested in your house. The more information buyers have, the better they will be able to make a decision about purchasing a house. The argument against this method, however, is that if too much information is given, buyers may not have a reason to call you. They think they already know all there is to know about your house, when, in fact, there may be many more things you could tell them about it. The second school of thought is that most of the people who take the flyers are nosy neighbors who just want to see how much you are selling your house for. As such, there is really no benefit derived from making information available in a box attached to the sign in your front yard. While it is true that many of your neighbors who may not be personally interested in buying your house will take a flyer, they may know of someone who is looking for a house.

So the question remains, do you need an information box attached to the sign in your front yard to make flyers available to anyone who might be interested? As a licensed real estate broker, I personally do not use information boxes for the many houses that I have for sale at any given time. I prefer instead to have potential buyers call the telephone number on the sign so that one of my sales agents can personally help them. If the house they have called on doesn't fit their particular needs, we can help them find another one. Furthermore, I'm able to generate inquiries and sales leads from an entire network of real estate agents who participate in the MLS. Your situation is different, however, in that you are not going to try to sell any house but your own, and you are not likely to have other real estate agents bringing buyers to you. So for individuals selling houses on their own, it's probably better to err on the side of making flyers available to as many people as possible, including the nosy neighbors!

How to Use an Open House to Sell Your House

The term *open house* refers to a small block of time, usually on a weekend, in which your house is open to the general public for the purpose of previewing it. As the host, you should prepare your house by making certain that it is clean and neat. You also may want to consider having some light refreshments such as cookies or a vegetable tray available for guests touring your house. If you serve punch, I recommend a drink that is clear rather than something like a red fruit punch. You don't want to take any chances with spills on your newly cleaned flooring, especially the carpet! If you like baking, homemade cookies are a good idea, too. The smell of fresh cookies baking in the oven creates an inviting aroma that's simply irresistible.

According to the NAR study, fully 48 percent of buyers used open houses as a method of gathering information about homes. Holding an open house is a good way of getting several would-be buyers to tour your house at the same time. The primary advantage of this is that instead of scheduling, say, five buyers to come through your house at different times throughout the week, you can schedule them all at the same time by providing them with a specified window of time. Open houses are most often advertised in local newspapers and real estate magazines and on signs. They should be held on the weekend in the afternoon for no more than two to three hours. Limiting the open house to no more than two or three hours increases the possibility that some buyers will be there at the same time. Having a house full of buyers is a very effective way of creating urgency among them, especially if they hear other buyers making favorable comments about your house. No one likes to miss out on a good deal. The presence of other buyers can get people out of the "We want to think about it" mode and into the "We'll take it!" mode because they're afraid that if they don't act soon, they'll miss out on the opportunity to buy.

An open house is also good for the buyer who just wants to tour your home without the pressure of having you hover over them. For example, when buyers call during the week to schedule an appointment with you, they know that they are dealing directly with the seller rather than an unbiased third party, such as a real estate agent. When buyers tour a house with an agent, they are free to comment on likes and dislikes without any pressure, but when they tour a house with the seller, it's a different story. In many instances, the buyer may not feel as comfortable sharing his or her objections directly with the seller. An open house environment affords buyers the opportunity to preview a house without the pressure of feeling like they have to buy. It's a nonthreatening environment in which they are free to look and ask questions without having to make a commitment.

How to Use Networking to Help Sell Your House

If you're like most people, you are probably already plugged into a large network of people who can help sell your house. These people include family members, friends, neighbors, business associates, and many more who may know of someone looking for a house to buy. The idea is to spread the word to as many people as you possibly can. The more people who know your house is for sale, the better chance you have of selling it. Following is a checklist of just a few of the many people you probably already know who can help sell your house.

- ☐ Business and work associates
- ☐ Family doctor
- ☐ Dentist
- ☐ Friends and neighbors
- ☐ Family members
- ☐ Church members
- ☐ Chamber of Commerce members
- ☐ Home owner's association members
- ☐ Post office employees
- ☐ Retail store employees
- ☐ Grocery store employees

- ☐ Restaurants
- ☐ Delivery services
- ☐ Bakery employees
- ☐ Beautician
- ☐ Nail salon employees
- ☐ Athletic club members and employees
- ☐ School functions, including sports, band, choir, and drama events.

How to Use Flyers to Help Sell Your House

I recommend preparing a one-page flyer that outlines the features and benefits of your house and distributing it to as many people as you possibly can, including those listed in the previous section on networking. Flyers can be posted just about anywhere you can think of, including grocery stores, church bulletin boards, office buildings, convenience stores, and the local pizza parlor. One advantage of using flyers is that a lot of information can be provided on them, including a photo of the house. Also, copies are fairly inexpensive to make, so using flyers won't cost you much. You can also use both sides of the flyer if you like. For example, one side of the flyer can be used to illustrate both interior and exterior photos, while the other side of the flyer can be used to provide pertinent information about your house. Be sure to list or describe those features that are especially different or unique about your house. In other words, what is it about your house that may be a strong selling point and makes it different from other houses that are for sale? Does it have new updates such as flooring and paint? Does it have a deck or a swimming pool? Does it have a fireplace or central air conditioning? Although it's a good idea to be thorough, be careful not to overdo it. You want readers to have a reason to call so that you can personally sell them on how wonderful your house is. In other words, be descriptive but, at the same time, leave something to the imagination. Following is a list of some of the information that should be included on your flyer.

- Interior and exterior photos
- Street address
- Price
- Number of bedrooms and bathrooms
- Size of garage: two-car, three-car, etc.

- Other special rooms such as a dining room or study
- Kitchen features such as an island, appliances, type of cabinetry
- Information about the heating, ventilation, and air conditioning systems
- Type and number of fireplaces, if applicable
- Information about the basement or other type of foundation
- Exterior features such as a deck, patio, swimming pool, storage shed
- Information about the yard, including landscaping, fencing, and size
- Information about the area, including school district, shopping, golf courses, lakes, etc.

In summary, while there are many ways to advertise your house, the seven methods discussed in this chapter are all highly effective. The study conducted by the National Association of Realtors is beneficial to sellers in that it uses actual data gathered from buyers to learn what sources they use in gathering information. By understanding where buyers look for information, the study helps sellers know how to make the most effective use of their marketing budgets. According to the study, 65 percent of all buyers use the Internet as a primary information source, 49 percent search newspapers, 35 percent use industry-specific real estate magazines, 69 percent use yard signs, and 48 percent say they attend open houses. In addition to those five sources, we have two more: networking with family, friends, and associates, and distributing flyers. This gives you a total of seven highly effective ways to market your house! Keep in mind that the more people who know your house is for sale, the more potential buyers you will have for it, and the more potential buyers you have for it, the quicker it will sell for top dollar.

7

Discount Brokerage Services: How to Co-op with Agents and Have the Buyer Pay the Commission

In Chapter 1, we discussed primary and secondary objectives for anyone wanting to sell his or her house. The primary objective for most homeowners who place their houses on the market is none other than to get their houses sold as close to full market value as possible. A secondary objective for many homeowners, especially those desiring to sell their own houses, is to save money in the process to minimize the cost of selling, which in turn will maximize the net return to them. If homeowners can achieve both of these objectives at the same time, then so much the better. One way to accomplish this is by using the services offered by agents and brokers on an à la carte basis. Many real estate companies today offer a choice of discounted brokerage services or fee-for-service agents who allow sellers to pick and choose only the services they need or want. Discounted services make it possible for the FSBO to sell his or her own house, while at the same time greatly expanding the pool of potential buyers. In this chapter, we'll discuss the advantages and disadvantages of using discount brokers and fee-for-service agents, some of the important services they offer, and, finally, how to have the buyer pay for them.

Discount Brokerage Services and Fee-for-Service Agents

In most areas throughout the nation, the average commission ranges from 5 percent to about 7 percent. The commission rates are not regulated by law, but are instead what the market will bear in any given area. Like other companies, brokerage firms must balance profits with a competitive price structure to stay in business. If a real estate company raises its rates too high, a competitor will come in and undercut it by offering similar services at a lower rate. Conversely, if a real estate company lowers its rates too much, then it will not be able to generate enough revenue to cover all of the expenses and still have a profit at the end of the day. In this capitalistic environment, it is the free-market forces that drive commission rates. This principle applies to almost all businesses that don't fall under heavy government regulation, including retailers. The success of mega-retailers like Wal-Mart is driven by two primary forces. The first is advances in technology that enable the company to be more competitive and thereby allow it to pass on the savings in the form of lower prices to its customers. The second is the willingness of the company to pass on the savings to its customers and operate on thinner profit margins, rather than attempting to keep the cost savings for themselves. By operating on lower margins and passing on the savings to consumers, Wal-Mart has been able to increase its total sales volume significantly, thereby enabling it to increase its overall level of profitability.

The underlying business philosophy of discount brokerage services is much the same as the highly successful Wal-Mart model. By offering services at a reduced rate, real estate companies hope to make up on volume what they sacrifice in margin. Much like Wal-Mart, if a brokerage firm can lure customers away from other real estate firms by offering lower rates to them, it will hopefully be able to increase the firm's overall profitability by representing even more customers. In other words, it hopes to make up the profits that are lost through lower commission rates through increased volume

Discounts offered by brokers vary widely and can be based on any number of factors or conditions. For example, if the average commission in a particular area is 3 percent, a discount broker may offer a range of discounts to sellers, depending on the level of service they desire. A broker may charge 1 percent to the seller for placing his or her house in the MLS and nothing more, 2 percent for placing the house in the MLS and representing the seller during the negotiation and contract period, and 2.5 percent for all of these services, plus advertising in several publications. These commission rates are only on the selling broker's side. If another agent brings a buyer, that agent will expect to get paid a full 3 percent commission. So, in effect, the discount fees in this example can range from as low as 1 percent, if there is no buyer's agent involved, to as high as 5.5 percent, if there is a buyer's agent present.

Fee-for-service agents work much the same way as discount brokerage firms—that is, by offering services à la carte rather than all or nothing. The primary difference is that the services are priced individually. It's much like going grocery shopping. If you want bananas, you put some in your basket and pay for them when you get to the register. If you want milk, you grab a gallon or two and pay for it when you get to the register. For those items you don't want, you simply leave them on the shelf for someone else. After you're all finished shopping, you pay only for those items in your cart and nothing more.

One primary difference between fee-for-service agents and discount brokers is that the fee-for-service items are typically paid for at the time they are used. Fee-for-service items are priced individually at a flat fee rather than on a percentage basis. For example, the agent might charge $600 to place your house in the MLS until it sells, and another $1,000 to represent you while negotiating with a buyer and making sure the purchase agreement gets filled out correctly. The advantage of using a flat rate fee structure is that services are purchased only as they are needed, for a set fee. The more expensive the house that's being sold, the lower the effective percentage is. Let's look at an example using two houses, one priced at $100,000 and the other priced at $200,000. Assume the fee for listing each house in the MLS is $600.

$$\$600/\$100,000 = 0.60\%$$
$$\$600/\$200,000 = 0.30\%$$

So, although the fee is $600 in both examples, it is lower as a percentage of sales price in the house selling for $200,000. One disadvantage of paying for the MLS service at the time it is used is that, if your house doesn't sell, you're out $600. The fee is considered *earned* at the time the services are rendered and is therefore not refundable just because your house didn't sell.

Unlike the fee-for-service agents, discount brokers who operate on a percentage commission basis don't get paid unless the customer's house sells. If the house doesn't sell, the broker doesn't get paid because commissions are not considered earned until the broker fulfills his or her obligation under the listing agreement. The advantage of this method to you is that there are no out-of-pocket costs up front. The only time you have to pay a commission is if your house sells. The commission would then be taken out of the proceeds at closing. The disadvantage of this method is that the fee is typically based on a percentage of the sales price rather than a previously set flat rate—this is oftentimes higher than the flat fee pricing structure. Using the previous example of two houses selling for $100,000 and $200,000, respectively, a discount broker who charges 1 percent for listing these houses would collect the following amounts in the event these houses were sold.

$$\$100,000 \times 1\% = \$1,000$$
$$\$200,000 \times 1\% = \$2,000$$

There is an obvious trade-off in using one rate structure over the other. You can pay up front at what is likely to be a lower rate as a percentage of the sales price and possibly not sell your house, or you can be prepared to pay a higher rate as a percentage of the sales price if your house does sell. If you are confident that your house is priced correctly and should have no problem selling in your market environment, then it probably makes sense to pay the lower rate in advance and not have to worry about paying a higher fee at the closing.

How to Sell Your House Faster Using This Important Service

The Multiple Listing Service, or MLS, is unquestionably the best way to get the most exposure for a seller's house. With technological advances and the advent of the Internet, the MLS acts as a virtual database of properties for sale that can be accessed from almost anywhere. There are literally thousands of real estate agents who use this service each day to search for properties that are for sale for their clients. Sellers who place their houses in the MLS can get immediate exposure, not only to buyers in their specific vicinity, but also to buyers from all parts of the country who may be interested in that particular area.

In many areas, for those agents who are also members of the National Association of Realtors, or NAR, the seller's property is automatically listed in what is perhaps the world's largest single database of properties for sale. The database is maintained on the Internet at www.realtor.com and can be accessed by anyone, whether he or she is a licensed agent or not. By allowing buyers to shop for properties anywhere in the nation at the click of a mouse button, realtor.com gives sellers access to potentially hundreds of thousands of buyers for a very nominal cost. As an example, it just so happens that one of my sales agents is working this very day with a family from Illinois that found several of our homes for sale on realtor.com. My sales agent has corresponded with them by e-mail, regular postal mail, and the telephone. The family is relocating to Michigan from Illinois and needs a house within the next 30 days. Two days ago, they loaded up the entire family, drove to Michigan, and spent the afternoon with my sales agent looking at the homes we have available for sale. The family has narrowed its selection down to one house in particular, and we are expecting a full price offer on it today. Without this invaluable service, the family would have had to resort to the more traditional method of locating a house in an area it has little knowledge of—contacting a local real estate agent who is familiar with the area.

The FSBO's Marketing and Sales Checklist

The process of getting a house placed in the MLS is relatively easy. Information is taken from a setup sheet that agents use to record data on and, in many cases, entered directly into the system through the Internet. The new listing is then made available on the MLS, usually within 24 hours. The following checklist is a partial list of the types of data that are entered into the MLS for each property.

- [ ] Property address, including street, city or town, state, and Zip code
- [ ] Legal address
- [ ] County
- [ ] Sales price
- [ ] Square feet
- [ ] Year of construction
- [ ] Number of stories or levels: one story, story and a half, two story, tri-level, etc.
- [ ] Description of rooms, including type of room (kitchen, bathroom, bedroom, etc.) and size
- [ ] School district
- [ ] Lot size
- [ ] Broker and agent contact information
- [ ] Listing date
- [ ] Status of the property: available, pending, sold, expired, withdrawn, etc.
- [ ] Type of property: single family, multifamily, commercial, vacant land
- [ ] Type of foundation: slab, crawl space, or basement
- [ ] If a basement foundation, characteristics such as daylight, walkout, finished, or unfinished

Once the data is entered into the MLS, agents who have access to the system can then search on any number of fields to pull up properties that match their specific criteria. As a member of the Flint Area Associations of Realtors, or FAAR, I can pull up information from the association's MLS system, known as Kinnexus, by simply keying in the appropriate criteria for the type of property I am looking for. Let's look at an example. I could enter the criteria found in Table 7.1 to find a particular house for a client.

Within seconds, the system would then return to me all available properties for sale that match the specified criteria. I could then view the

Table 7.1

Field Description	Minimum	Maximum
Price	$200,000	$250,000
Square feet	1,800	None
School district	Grand Blanc	
Foundation	Walkout basement	
Bedrooms	3	4
Lot size	1 acre	5 acres
Year built	2005	None

list, print it out, or e-mail it to my client. As previously mentioned, only licensed agents or members of the realtor's association have access to the MLS. Although the general public cannot use this system to locate houses, similar searches can be performed on realtor.com. This is the tool the family from Illinois that was described in the earlier example used to find new homes in Michigan. The bottom line is that by using either a fee-for-service agent or a discount brokerage company to list your house for sale in the MLS and on realtor.com, you can gain immediate exposure to literally thousands of potential buyers.

How to Get the Buyer to Help Pay for These Services

The cost to list your house in the MLS can range from as little as a few hundred dollars, using a fee-for-service agent, to as much as an additional 3 percent if an agent brings the client to buy your house. This is known as a co-op, which means you are cooperating with a buyer's agent by agreeing to pay him or her a commission for bringing a purchaser to you. So, on a house selling for $150,000, a co-op fee of 3 percent represents an additional $4,500 off the bottom line. There are several ways to compensate for this additional cost. One way is to pass the entire cost to the buyer by simply adjusting the price of the house upward enough to offset the commission. While increasing the price is possible to do, doing so will, in large part, depend on the strength of the real estate market in your area. If the sales activity is strong enough to support a price increase to cover the commission, then by all means go ahead and raise the price. Be careful when doing so, however, as maintaining the proper balance between your sales price and what the market will bear is a delicate process.

If your house is already priced at the upper end of the market, or if sales in your area are not as robust as other areas, then passing the entire cost of the commission through to the buyer by increasing the sales price 3 percent may not be a viable option. An alternative to passing the full 3 percent through to the buyer is to pass half of the cost through instead. By increasing the sales price 1.5 percent, you run less risk of overpricing your house in a competitive market environment. With this alternative, you and the buyer share equally in the added cost of the commission while minimizing the chance of overpricing your house.

One additional option you may want to consider is to have the sales agent pay part of the commission. That's right. The sales agent can be given the opportunity to contribute to his or her own commission. Here's how it works. Let's assume the agent's commission is 3 percent. If you pay 1 percent, the buyer pays 1 percent, and the agent pays 1 percent, then the sum of these is 3 percent. I know, I know. You're wondering how the agent can pay for his or her own commission. The answer is by contributing 1 percent of the total 3 percent, which effectively means the agent is willing to forgive, or waive, 1 percent of his or her commission and work for a total of 2 percent instead. So by increasing the price of the house enough to cover 1 percent of the commission, the buyer is paying for 1 percent. By being willing to accept 1 percent less for the net proceeds on the sale of the house, you are paying for 1 percent of the commission. And, finally, by agreeing to accept 2 percent on the sale of your house, the agent is paying for 1 percent of the commission.

Perceived Costs versus Real Costs

While there is a very real cost associated with agent services, the argument could be made that in reality these services cost you nothing. In fact, they can even help you save money. You ask, "How can this be?" The answer lies in the increased number of buyers that may potentially be brought to you through the greatly increased exposure of being listed on the MLS. The more buyers there are that are interested in your house, the more likely you are able to get full price for it. As an example, if you had been trying to sell your house without using the MLS for six months before finally getting an offer, there's a good chance that you may have lowered the price on your house already. You may furthermore be more inclined to accept less for your house, regardless of what the current asking price was. On the other hand, if your house was listed in the MLS and you had two or three buyers interested in it within the first 45 days, you would be greatly encouraged by the response and would therefore be more likely to stand firm on the asking price. In this example, you would most likely have come out ahead by using a fee-for-service agent or discount brokerage firm.

In summary, remember that your primary goal is to get your house sold for as close to full market price as possible. While some of you may not be in any hurry to sell, others of you will need to sell fairly quickly. As an FSBO, a goal secondary to selling your house is keeping as much of the proceeds from the sale as possible by minimizing expenses. One of the best ways to achieve both of these goals is by using a discount broker or a fee-for-service agent to place your house in the Multiple Listing Service. Although these services do cost money, the costs may be more perceived than real and may or may not reduce the net proceeds to you.

8

Home Presentation: How to Show Your Home to Qualified Buyers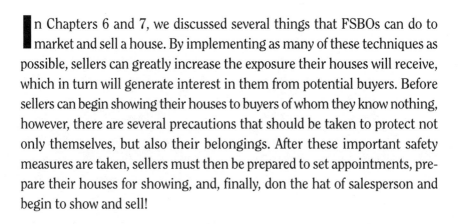

In Chapters 6 and 7, we discussed several things that FSBOs can do to market and sell a house. By implementing as many of these techniques as possible, sellers can greatly increase the exposure their houses will receive, which in turn will generate interest in them from potential buyers. Before sellers can begin showing their houses to buyers of whom they know nothing, however, there are several precautions that should be taken to protect not only themselves, but also their belongings. After these important safety measures are taken, sellers must then be prepared to set appointments, prepare their houses for showing, and, finally, don the hat of salesperson and begin to show and sell!

Safety First

Although your primary objective is to get your house sold for as close to full market value as possible, it is even more important to take certain precautionary steps to safeguard not only your belongings, but yourself as well. While most people tend to be fairly trusting of others, you unfortunately don't have that luxury when it comes to opening up your house to someone who is a complete stranger. To help reduce the risk of opening up your house to a would-be perpetrator, start by asking callers for basic information about themselves before agreeing to show your house. Use the following checklist as a minimum guideline to gather information about visitors.

- [ ] Full name
- [ ] Current address
- [ ] Telephone number
- [ ] Place of employment
- [ ] Driver's license number and state of issuance
- [ ] Persons who will also come to preview your house—spouse, children, parents, aunts, uncles, etc.

Any buyers who are serious about purchasing your house should be willing to provide this information, especially their names, addresses, and telephone numbers. With that information alone, you should be able to verify whether or not they are who they say they are by simply looking them up in the phone book. If the telephone number happens to be unlisted, you can at least call them back to confirm the number they gave you. If a buyer gives you false information, then this should serve as a red flag either to cancel the appointment if possible or not answer the door when he or she arrives. Knowing the buyers' employers can be helpful because that gives you one more source that can confirm they are who they say they are. For example, you can call a buyer's place of employment and simply verify that he works there. If the buyer is a criminal, then it's quite possible he wouldn't be able to provide you with legitimate information about an employer because he is probably not employed. You may get some resistance from buyers when you ask for their driver's license numbers. Just explain to them that if they were coming with a real estate agent, the agent would not only require the license number, but would also require an actual photocopy of the license. Practically every day real estate agents face the same risk of showing houses to people they know nothing about. Obtaining a copy of driver's licenses and filing them at the broker's office is the requisite policy for many agencies. The bottom line is that you are responsible for your own safety, so if you meet any kind of resistance from a buyer when asking for this information, it may be better to pass on allowing him or her to enter into your house.

Another safety precaution you should take when showing your house to potential buyers is always to make sure there is more than one person at home. This is especially true if you are a woman, and doubly true if you are a woman showing your house to a man. If you are married, always try to arrange to have your spouse home during a showing. A would-be perpetrator is much less likely to try anything if there is more than one person home. If you live by yourself and no family member is available, have a friend or neighbor come over while you are showing your house. If a neighbor is at home, but is not available to come over, you could arrange to have her keep an eye on your house while you are showing it. You may even want to prearrange a signal with neighbors if you are in trouble. For example, turning the front porch light on could serve as a signal to your neighbor to call the police immediately. Another suggestion is to carry the telephone handset around the house with you while showing it, so again, if you get into trouble, you can dial 911 immediately. One additional safety precaution is to show your house during daylight hours whenever possible. During the winter season when the days are shorter, this may not always be possible, especially if someone wants to see your house in the evening after they leave work. While none of these methods can completely guarantee your safety, using one or more of them can most assuredly help minimize the risk of a criminal act against you and your family.

After following the suggested safety precautions to safeguard yourself, it's time to think about safeguarding whatever valuables you have in your house, especially those items that are small and could easily be slipped into a pocket without being detected. If you have a safe in your house, I recommend securing valuables such as jewelry, watches, rare coins, and extra cash in it. Any items that are small and of considerable value should be stored away for safekeeping because you never know what somebody may decide to walk off with. It's better to put things away and minimize the risk of their being stolen than it is to take any chances with strangers about whom you know very little.

Show Your House by Appointment Only

If you've ever sold a house before, I'm sure you know how inconvenient it can be at times to have to drop everything and do a quick clean up of your house just to let some stranger you may never see again walk through it. Showing your house by appointment only will help reduce some of the stress related to the sales process and also give you the time you need to verify the accuracy of the information prospective buyers have provided you with. Most, but not all, buyers understand this rule as a simple courtesy. After all, if they are looking at houses with a real estate agent who must call ahead to schedule an appointment, why should they mind calling you to do the same? If you intend to show your house by appointment only, then you need to make buyers aware of this by making sure that information is included on your sign, on your flyers, and most other forms of advertising you are doing.

When prospective buyers do call for an appointment, try to be as accommodating as possible. Sometimes this may mean showing your house on very short notice. If you adopt this mindset from the beginning, however, you will be mentally prepared ahead of time to deal with it. Remember that, in today's fast food society, consumers are by and large impatient. We don't like standing in lines; we get upset if we have to wait more than a couple of minutes in a drive-through lane at a restaurant; and we honk the horn at the driver in front of us if he's not prepared to hit the accelerator the second the traffic light turns green. Home buyers can be the same way at times, especially if they are driving through your neighborhood on a Saturday afternoon and see the sign in your front yard. Yes, that's right, the same one that says in large, bold letters, "Shown by Appointment Only." While some passersby will respect this by writing down the number and calling later, others will want to see it now.

So the question arises, "How do you handle the individual who may or may not be a legitimate buyer who wants to see your house on very short notice? Most people today have cell phones, so they may very well be parked right in front of your house calling the number on the sign. If your house is in order and you have the time to show it at that moment, then use the Safety First checklist rules previously discussed in this chapter. Although you may or may not be able to verify all of the information, at least you will be able to establish a level of comfort with the buyer by asking these questions and getting a sense of whether or not they resist giving it to you. One tactic you can use to verify the information and get a little extra time is to ask the buyer politely to return in 15 or 20 minutes. This way the buyer can drive around the neighborhood for a few minutes while you are verifying the information given to you. Also, be sure to ask the buyer if he or she is alone, or if someone is with him or her. You should be able to peek through the blinds to confirm whether or not he or she is alone. If there is a couple outside with several children, then there's a good chance that it's safe to let them in. If it is a man who is by himself, and you are a woman who is alone, I strongly suggest you follow the previously mentioned safety guidelines by deferring the showing until a later time. Also, if it's already dark outside, then you have no way of confirming who is in the car, so it may be better to put them off by asking them to come at a later time. On the other hand, if you are not at home alone and there are others there with you, then it's probably safe to proceed with showing your house. While it is important to follow these general safety guidelines, you must also let common sense prevail.

Home Preparation Checklist

Before a prospective buyer ever enters your house, there are several steps you should take to prepare it. Perhaps the most important thing to remember is that previewing a house is much more than a visual experience. For example, when a couple comes to look at a house, they are thinking not only about themselves, but about their children. They are thinking about where the kids will play, where they will sleep, where they will go to school, and who their friends will be. The decision to move into a new house takes far more into consideration than just the bricks and sticks. It is an emotional experience that affects the very core of the human psyche. With this in mind, it is essential to focus on not only the visual appearance of your house, but its total environment—that is to say, those elements that affect the human senses. These include our senses of sight, smell, sound, touch, and taste. By providing buyers with a sensory-rich experience, your house is far more likely to appeal to them than those houses they have looked at which have provided nothing more than a superficial visual encounter. Don't get me wrong.

Home Presentation

A positive visual experience is essential to showing your house successfully, but it only gives buyers a one-dimensional view of your house. It is the combination of two or more sensory elements that help set your house apart. Let's now take a more in-depth look at the five senses and how you can use them to provide a multidimensional shopping experience for buyers previewing your house.

Sense 1: Sight

The overriding premise to keep in mind for the sense of sight checklist is the general cleanliness of your house. This doesn't mean it has to be 100 percent perfect. Your house should be clean, but not necessarily to the extent that it looks like a museum. In other words, it should look lived in.

- Exterior: Lawn should be mowed during spring and summer months, snow shoveled off walks and drives in winter months (see Chapter 2 for complete list of exterior improvements).
- Interior: Start by making sure your house is bright and cheery, not dark and dreary. This means opening up the blinds or shades and turning on the lights throughout the house.
- Floors: Vacuum carpets, rugs and floors throughout the house.
- Kitchen: Make sure sink is empty, countertops are clutter-free, dishes are put away, and floor is clean.
- Family room: No clutter on the floor, end tables neat and clean, television off.
- Bedrooms: Beds made, dirty clothes picked up off floor, kids' toys put away if not being used.
- Bathrooms: Dirty clothes and towels picked up, vanity tops and mirrors clean.
- General cleanliness: Check to ensure that any other rooms your house may have are relatively clean and clutter free.

Sense 2: Smell

It's important to be aware of the odors in your house because they can have either a negative or positive effect on buyers. What may be a pleasant odor to one person, however, may not be so pleasant to another person. For example, while some people love the rich aroma given off by fresh coffee, others may not care for it all, especially those who don't drink it. The trick is how to determine what distinguishes a pleasant odor from an unpleasant one. As a general rule, rather than try to distinguish differences between pleasant and unpleasant odors, your best bet is to maintain an *odor neutral environment*. An odor neutral environment is one in which you can't detect any smell at all. One of the main problems with this, however, is that it is sometimes difficult for people to tell when they have an odor in their own homes. This is because people become accustomed to certain odors and, to them, those odors begin to smell perfectly normal. Over time, odors can even become almost imperceptible, and therefore odor neutral, to them because they are so accustomed to them.

Let's look at an example. A man who has smoked cigarettes every day for the past 20 years is not likely to detect the strong odor of smoke and nicotine when he enters his house because he has grown used to it over the years. It's the way his house smells and, to him, his house smells perfectly normal. A nonsmoker, on the other hand, entering this man's house will immediately notice the odor and may even find the odor to be quite offensive. If the smoker is trying to sell his house to a nonsmoker, he may have a problem. My advice is to have as much of the nicotine smell removed as possible by having the carpets, drapes, curtains, and upholstery cleaned, since they tend to absorb odors.

When preparing your house to show, it's best to maintain as close to an odor neutral environment as possible. It's okay to spray an air freshener with a light fragrance shortly before a buyer comes to see your house, but be careful not to overdo it. It's kind of like the guy you know down the hall at the office who always wears too much cologne. He thinks he smells great, but everyone else is keeping their distance.

Sense 3: Sound

Our sense of sound reveals a great deal about the environment around us. Just this morning I was awakened by my wife who asked if I could hear "that sound" outside. "It sounds like a cricket," she said. I first responded by telling her that no, I couldn't hear the sound outside because I was asleep. After listening for a brief moment, I said, "That's not a cricket. It's a bird chirping." I drifted back off to sleep thinking to myself, "At last . . . spring is finally here . . ." After a long, hard winter, the sound of birds happily chirping outside brings great joy to me, because I know that spring has truly arrived. For me this sound created a happy, peaceful feeling. Our sense of sound can bring great pleasure to us. For example, we hear the sound of happy children playing together, or a baby gleefully cooing, or even a roller coaster full of thrill seekers screaming shrills of delight. In addition to alerting us to pleasurable sounds, our sense of sound also alerts us to sounds that are unpleasant. For example, we hear the sound of children quarreling with one another, or a baby incessantly crying, or people who are waiting in a long line to ride the roller coaster and are growing increasingly impatient.

Sounds can evoke a wide range of feelings and emotions within us. A neighbor's barking dog may cause us to feel resentment toward her. A snake hissing nearby may strike a chord of fear. Voices raised in an argumentative tone can result in feelings of anger. A crowd cheering at a basketball game evokes excitement. You get the idea. When preparing to show your house to prospective buyers, make sure the sounds they hear are friendly, happy sounds. Turn the television off if possible. If you have little children who are watching a program, that's okay. Just make sure the volume isn't set too loud. If you have older teenagers who like to "rock out" to one of their favorite music groups, make sure they aren't rocking out when buyers are coming through. Noises in the background send imperceptible signals to the buyer's subconscious mind. For example, the sound of laughter from happy children playing in the background is much better than the sound of gunfire erupting from the television. Try to maintain a positive, happy, and uplifting environment in your house when showing it to buyers by being aware of the sounds they may hear.

Sense 4: Touch

Our fourth sense is the sense of touch and pertains primarily to the way our bodies feel when we are indoors. The sense of touch, as it relates to showing your house, centers around the ambient air temperature. In other words, depending on what temperature your thermostat is set at, a person may feel too warm, too cool, or just right. In the winter, it's best to keep your house warm and cozy so that buyers feel comfortable while inside. Also, if your house has a fireplace in it, it's a good idea to light it while showing the house. Not only will it generate additional heat, but it will also help in creating a warm and inviting atmosphere. It's better to err on the side of being a little too warm rather than too cold. If the buyer is too cold, for example, she may end up wanting to leave just so that she can get warmed up in the car. Maintaining the proper temperature in the warmer months is equally as important. Don't overdo it by turning your house into a giant refrigerator, but do keep it pleasantly cool for buyers as they walk through your house, especially on those days that are exceptionally warm. It will be a welcome relief from the heat outdoors and will likely tempt buyers to stay longer.

Sense 5: Taste

Our fifth sense is the sense of taste. It is closely related to the sense of smell. To allow buyers to experience the sense of taste while they are in your house, you may consider having light refreshments available for them after they have toured it. This gives you the opportunity to visit with them in a more relaxed setting and obtain feedback from them about your house. Keeping the discussion lighthearted over a delicious snack can help set the buyers at ease and help them to feel more comfortable sharing with you what their specific needs are. This informal and casual dialogue also helps to build trust with the buyer, thereby allowing them to open up to you a little more. I suggest keeping the refreshments simple, something like a veggie tray, cookies, and clear colored punch. Freshly baked chocolate chip cookies are one of my favorites and would probably be a big hit for most buyers who have their children with them. Although the aroma of freshly baked cookies violates our odor neutral rule, this is one odor that I believe most people enjoy.

Time to Show and Sell

Now that your house has been fully prepared to appeal to two or more of the five senses, it's time to show and sell! You are more qualified to sell your house than anyone else because if you're like most people, you have probably spent the last several years living in it. You are the key to sharing with others what it is about your house that makes it special, what sets it apart and makes it different from all other houses. There are four simple yet important rules you should follow when showing your house to buyers. They include giving the buyer plenty of space, being able to point out the features and benefits of your house, focusing on its positive attributes, and, finally, making the experience fun.

Rule 1: Give the Buyer Space

The first rule to follow when showing your house is to give the buyer plenty of space. This doesn't mean that you should allow buyers to walk freely through your house unaccompanied, especially if it their first time to preview it. Remember that they are strangers, and even though you have taken certain precautionary measures to verify who they are, you still don't really know them. Giving buyers plenty of space means to walk with them and not on top of them as they are viewing your house. You don't want to come across as being too overbearing by trying to make a hard sale. Your job is to provide information and to be prepared to answer questions.

Rule 2: Features and Benefits

The second rule for showing your house is to be prepared to point out its features and benefits. Most areas in your house will have certain items that you especially enjoy. That item is a feature, and the enjoyment or functionality of it is the benefit. For example, the kitchen in my house has a center island with an electrical outlet mounted on the side. I use the island on average two to three times a week to make smoothies. My ritual includes getting out the smoothie maker, plugging it into the outlet mounted on the center island, and whipping up a batch of smoothies mixed with strawberries, pineapples, and bananas. If I were showing my house to a buyer, I would point out the center island (the feature) and then share with him how handy it is to have and how much I enjoy making smoothies on it (the benefit). Table 8.1 lists five examples of features and benefits. You should be able to list several more for your house.

Rule 3: Accentuate the Positive

The third rule to remember when showing your house to buyers is to be sure and focus on its strengths and not its weaknesses. In other words, accentuate the positive, not the negative. Let me share with you a prime example of what *not* to do. Just two weeks ago, I went to visit a client about listing her house for sale. She and her husband had just purchased one of our brand new Symphony Homes and had requested that I help her sell her

Table 8.1

Feature	Benefit
Large backyard	Great place for kids to play
Deck or patio	Relaxing area to grill out and entertain friends
Three-car garage	Plenty of space to park the cars and extra room to store things
Master bathroom	Spacious design, relaxing tub, separate shower stall for added convenience
Family room	Plenty of room for furniture and entertainment center

house. Mrs. X was a somewhat cantankerous woman, and it seemed that pretty much everything about life rubbed her the wrong way. When I went to look at her house, she spent nearly a full hour telling me all the things that she didn't like about it and all of the reasons she wanted to move. She didn't like the neighbor across the street because he didn't have his lawn in yet. She didn't like the neighbor next to her because she did have her lawn in, but didn't mow it regularly. She didn't like the other neighbor across the street because that woman left her blinds open, allowing others to see in at night. The list went on and on. Thank goodness Mrs. X asked me to sell her house for her and did not try to do so on her own. If she had, no buyers in their right minds would have purchased her house because she gave them every reason under the sun not to! When showing your house, give buyers reasons to want to live there by accentuating the positive, not the negative.

Rule 4: Make it Fun!

The fourth rule to remember when showing your house to buyers is to make it fun. In other words, make the previewing and buying experience an absolutely delightful one for your buyers. Although somewhat similar to Rule 3, Rule 4 takes the sales process a step further by not only accentuating the positive, but by maintaining an upbeat and lighthearted atmosphere as well. You want to do everything possible to help buyers feel like they are welcome, such as not acting put out because they came at an odd hour of the day. You should refrain from any form of communication that sends the wrong message to buyers. This includes both verbal and nonverbal signals, such as facial expressions, that may send the wrong message. Force yourself to smile because doing so will let buyers know you are happy to have them there and will also help to set them at ease. Buyers who feel at ease with you are more likely to trust you and will therefore feel more at ease buying your house. Keeping things lighthearted is the beginning of putting buyers in the proper frame of mind for taking that very important step—signing a purchase agreement.

In summary, remember that before you can sell your house, you have to have an effective marketing strategy that will generate phone calls from interested buyers. Before you can begin showing your house to them, however, you must take several safety precautions to help minimize the threat of perpetrators who may wish to harm you. Once you have followed the steps outlined in this chapter, you can then begin scheduling appointments. Be sure to prepare your house to appeal to as many of the buyers' senses as possible to create a sensory-rich environment for them. Finally, it's time to don the hat of salesperson and begin to show and sell!

9

Negotiating Strategies: How to Get What You Want without Giving Away the Farm

In the last chapter, we examined the process of scheduling appointments and showing your house to prospective buyers. In this chapter, we'll learn about knowing what to do with those buyers once they've shown up. Buyers will seldom come right out and tell you they're ready to purchase. As the seller, you must be prepared to listen for and observe both verbal and non-verbal clues. Trial closing questions can also be used along the way to gauge a buyer's readiness to take action. You'll also learn about how buyers float trial balloons, and how you can use them to your advantage to close the sale. We'll then discuss what to do if a buyer offers less than full price for your house, and how to go about making a counteroffer. Finally, we'll learn about contingencies and subject-to clauses, as well as the proper way to accept a buyer's earnest money deposit.

How to Use Verbal and Nonverbal Clues to Know If a Buyer Is Hot or Cold

Without coming right out and telling you directly, buyers typically give off indirect verbal and nonverbal clues about whether or not they like your house. Furthermore, the type and extent of questions they ask can also provide you with clues to how much the buyer likes or dislikes your house. One example of an indirect verbal clue is when a couple is previewing your house and one spouse turns to the other and comments, "Oh, this is nice, honey!" Or one spouse may comment quietly to the other something like, "This bedroom is too small for the kids. It'll never work." Listen carefully when possible to the dialog carried on between two or more people as they walk through your house and you'll be surprised at how much you can learn from them. Nonverbal clues can be just as powerful as indirect verbal clues and are given off through facial expressions and body language. For example, if you see a woman's face light up as she enters the kitchen, there's a good chance she likes it. On the other hand, if you detect a grimace on her face, look out because the kitchen is one of the most important rooms in the house, especially to a woman.

Other nonverbal signs to look for include buyers' hands as they walk through the house. For example, if they run their hands across a cabinet or countertop, that's generally a sign that they like it and are further admiring it. The hands are used to confirm what the eyes see and act as a secondary sense to support what a primary sense has already observed. Another excellent clue to look for is when buyers begin to mentally place their furniture in a room. For example, one spouse may comment to the other, "Honey, I think our sofa will fit perfectly against this wall." The other spouse may in turn respond by saying something like, "Yes, you're right! And I think there's just enough room on this wall for our entertainment center!"

In addition to verbal and nonverbal expressions of interest, you can also learn quite a bit from potential buyers by the extent and types of questions they ask. If a buyer walks through a house rather quickly without asking any questions, that's generally a good sign that she's not interested in it. On the other hand, if a buyer walks through a house taking his time and asking lots of questions, that's generally a good sign that he is genuinely interested in it. The buyer is attempting to ascertain within his own mind whether or not your house will meet his needs. By asking lots of questions, he is gathering the information necessary to make a proper determination. The more information you can provide the buyer with, the better he or she will be able to make a decision about whether or not your house is suitable. Following are just a few of the many questions you should be prepared to answer.

- Why are you selling your house?
- How many square feet is your house?
- How old is your house? What year was it built in?
- What size is the lot?
- How large is the family room?
- How many bedrooms and bathrooms are there?
- What are the room sizes of the bedrooms?
- What are your neighbors like? Do they have children? Do they have an outdoor pet? Are they easy to get along with?
- Where do you do most of your shopping?
- What schools would our children attend and where are they located?
- How much are the taxes?
- How much do your utility bills average each month?
- How old are the furnace and air conditioning systems?
- Are the blinds and drapes included with your house?
- What is that stain on the ceiling? Does the roof leak?
- How old are the kitchen appliances and do they work properly?
- Is there anything in the house that doesn't work properly?

By listening carefully to the buyers, you can assess their level of interest in your home. For example, if the buyers are genuinely excited about your home and have expressed a strong interest in it, you can use that information to your advantage because it provides you with a stronger point from which to negotiate. Buyers who are really excited about a particular house are generally willing to pay closer to full asking price than those who may be only somewhat interested. You can use that information to your advantage by negotiating as close to full price as possible. The same principle holds true for those buyers who express a degree of urgency in making a purchase decision. For example, a buyer who just sold her house and has only 30 days to find another one and close on it has a high degree of urgency and will therefore not be in as strong a position to bargain with you. If you know the seller must act quickly, use that information to your advantage by negotiating as close to full price as possible.

How to Use Trial Closing Questions to Gauge a Buyer's Readiness

Trial closing questions are designed to determine a buyer's likes and dislikes regarding a house, as well as his or her degree of readiness to take some type of action. In my many years of experience, buyers seldom come right out and tell you they are ready to buy. Very rare is the buyer who says, "I'll take it! Where do I sign?" If you're fortunate enough to have such a buyer, be prepared to have the sales agreement readily available and respond by saying, "Right here!" The purchase of a house is one of the largest financial decisions most people ever make and is not one that can be rushed. In fact, most buyers will not purchase on the first visit, but will instead come back two, three, or even four times before making a decision. You can begin to obtain feedback from the buyer by posing questions like, "How do you like the master bedroom and bathroom? Aren't they beautiful?" Or, "Isn't this a magnificent kitchen? Just look at all of these cabinets!" After asking a trial question, then it's time for you to be quiet. That's right, it's time for you to be quiet and listen carefully to how the buyer responds.

To test the buyer's readiness to purchase, you can ask questions that will help gauge where they are in the buying process. For example, you may ask a question like, "How soon are you folks wanting to move?" Their response can be quite revealing. If a couple states, for example, "Oh, we're not in any hurry. We need to sell our house first and we haven't even put it on the market yet," then this is a good indicator that their timing most likely does not match yours. On the other hand, if the couple responds, "We just sold our house and we have to find another one right away because we have to close on ours in 30 days," then you know you have a buyer who has an urgent need. You can then follow up your initial question with one that asks the buyer to take action. For example, you may tell the buyer something like, "Mr. Buyer, I can tell you and your wife really love this beautiful home. In fairness to you, I have had several families through the house earlier this week who have expressed an interest in it. In fact, one of them told me they would be back this weekend with their parents to look at the house one more time before making their final decision. Rather than have you run the risk of losing this beautiful home to someone else, I have all the paperwork right here for us to get started."

The next step is to slide the paperwork in front of them, hand them the pen, and say, "I just need your approval at the bottom of the form, and this lovely home is yours!" Buyers need you to ask them to buy. Rarely do they ask, "Where do I sign?" You must be prepared to show them where to sign. To some readers, this approach may sound a little pushy and may be outside of your comfort zone. If you don't ask the buyer to buy, however, there's a good chance he or she may not. This closing method is referred to as an *assumptive approach* because you are asking the buyer to purchase your house by assuming that he will. I have used it many times and can personally attest that is a very effective closing method. Rather than asking the buyer outright to purchase, you have instead assumed that he or she will. By using the assumptive approach, the buyer must now find a reason to tell you no. In other words, the burden is no longer on you, the seller, to ask for the sale, but is instead on the buyer to decline it. If the buyer says nothing, you can only assume he must be ready to purchase!

How to Use the Buyer's "Trial Balloon" to Close the Sale

Buyers often float what I refer to as *trial balloons*. The term *trial balloon* originated in 1782 with the launching of unmanned hot air balloons to test their ability to fly. These initial flights were intended to test the balloons to determine their potential usefulness for military purposes. The idea was to fly over the enemy's position and overcome its forces by penetrating what was considered to be an impregnable fortress surrounded by a very high wall. Although the term *trial balloon* is still widely used today, it seldom refers to a hot air balloon. The term does, however, share a similar meaning in that, when it is used, it most often refers to a trial or a test of something. Whether they are aware of it or not, buyers routinely float trial balloons with questions posed to the seller regarding price, such as, "Would you take $140,000 for your house instead of the $145,000 you are asking for it?" A buyer might also test your willingness to throw something in for free with a question like, "If I buy your house, would you be willing to pay all of the closing costs?" While there are many variations of the trial balloon, they all share one thing in common. The buyer is asking you to give up something without making any kind of commitment to you in return. As an active investor who buys and sells millions of dollars worth of real estate each year, I know this game all too well, and I play it to my advantage.

Here's how it works. Earlier this week one of my sales agents had a buyer stop by one of our model homes. The buyer, who was represented by her own real estate agent, wanted to know if we would accept $1,000 down as earnest money for one of our new houses that was about 30 days away from completion. My company's standard policy is to ask for 5 percent as an earnest money deposit. If the buyer doesn't have the required 5 percent, we will work with them in order to make the sale—within reason that is. In this particular instance, because the house was almost completed, I was willing to accept less than 5 percent. Instead of sharing my willingness to work with the buyer with no commitment on her part to me, I used this as an opportunity to close the sale by getting the buyer to make an offer. I told my sales agent to inform the buyer that I could not consider her offer of only $1,000 down unless it was in writing. Then, and only then, would I consider it. Experience has taught me that when a concession is made with no commitment on the part of the buyer, another concession is soon asked for. First the buyer wants to hold a $215,000 house with only $1,000, she wants you to discount it by $5,000, then she wants you to throw in free appliances, and so on and so on. You get the idea. My response is always the same. I tell buyers to "put it in writing" first, and then I will be happy to consider their offers. This method allows me to take the buyer's trial balloon and turn it into a very powerful closing technique. By the way, the buyer in this example did exactly as we suggested and put her offer in writing. My sales agent brought me a full price offer from the buyer the very next day. She put her proposal for $1,000 earnest money in writing, which I countered at $2,000, which she in turn accepted! In this example, we sold the house to the buyer using her own trial balloon by getting her to make a written commitment to us. As you begin to show your house to prospective buyers, use trial balloons as opportunities to convert them to firm offers and to get your house sold quickly!

What to Do If a Buyer Offers Less Than Full Asking Price

Before placing your house on the market for sale, you should determine the absolute lowest price that you are willing to accept. Once you have established that, you will know how to respond. You should note, however, that price isn't everything. There may be certain compensating factors in the buyer's offer that may allow you to accept less than your predetermined minimum price. For example, if the buyer has the ability to consummate the sale by closing in 30 days, that may be a better option for you and can potentially save you money, especially if you have already purchased another house. In general though, you should have a minimum price in mind that you are willing to accept beforehand so that you know how to respond when an offer comes in less than your asking price. Just be prepared to be flexible if necessary.

Once you have established a minimum price, recall from the previous section that before you consider any offer, it must be in writing. If the offer is merely a verbal one, get the buyer to put it in writing by telling him or her that you cannot consider the offer unless it is in writing. Once the offer is written, you can then use it as a point from which to begin negotiating. Whether you accept a buyer's offer that is less than full asking price is entirely up to you; however, there are several factors that may influence your decision. They include the strength of the market in your area, your need and degree of urgency to sell, how long your house has been available for sale, and whether the offer you have received is a realistic one or not.

If you live in an area where the market is strong and it only takes one to two months at the most to sell a house, then you may want to hold out for an offer that is closer to your asking price. On the other hand, if you live in an area where it can take six to twelve months to sell a house, then you will want to think very seriously about negotiating with the buyer to try to achieve a price and terms that both of you can agree to. Another factor to consider is how badly you need to sell your house. If you are not in any hurry to sell and have the luxury of staying in your house for as long as you want, then you may want to hold out for an offer that is closer to your full asking price. If, on the other hand, you just received a job promotion, are being transferred to another area, and have only a short time before starting your new job, you will likely want to consider working with the buyer to achieve a price and terms that are acceptable to both of you. Still another factor to consider is how long your house has been for sale relative to the average time of other houses. For example, if your house has been on the market for six months already, while most houses in your area are selling in only three months, it may be an indication that your house is overpriced. If that is the case, then it is probably a good idea to give serious consideration to an offer that is less than your full asking price.

Finally, one additional factor that must be considered when receiving an offer that is lower than your asking price is whether or not it is realistic. In other words, did the buyer present you with an offer that is so out of line with the market that, on its surface, it appears to be ridiculously low? I can't tell you how many low-ball offers I've received, not only on some of my houses, but on some of my apartment buildings as well. In situations like that I often don't even bother to respond because we are so far apart on price. I've learned over the years that if the buyer is serious, he or she will send over a second offer that is more in line with my asking price and, if not, then the buyer must not have been that interested to begin with. By not responding, I haven't wasted any of my time.

How to Make a Counteroffer

When a buyer presents a sales contract to you, he or she is making an *offer*. If you do not accept the buyer's offer exactly as it is written, but instead respond by making one or more changes to it, you are then making a *counteroffer*. Let's look at an example. If a buyer offers less money than the price you are asking, you can do one of three things: accept the buyer's offer exactly as it is, reject the buyer's offer by doing nothing, or make additional changes and submit a counteroffer back to the buyer. To counter the buyer's offering price, simply strike through the price on the contract and replace it with the price you are willing to accept. Each time a change is made to the contract it must be initialed, so when you line through the buyer's offering price and replace it with your own, you must initial the change. The contract is then submitted back to the buyer who can also do one of three things: accept your counteroffer by initialing the change, reject your counteroffer by doing nothing, or make additional changes and resubmit another counteroffer back to you.

Contingencies and Subject to Clauses

A *contingency* is a clause in a sales agreement used for the purpose of making the occurrence of one action dependent upon the occurrence of another action. In other words, it is language used within the contract that states that one action must occur before another action can occur. It is one condition that is *subject to* another condition. An example of one commonly used contingency is one that is based on the sale of the buyer's house. For example, you might receive an offer that is "contingent upon the sale of Purchaser's primary residence." This means that the buyer is only willing to purchase your house when and if her house sells. If the buyer's house does not sell, then she is under no obligation to purchase your house. Another commonly used contingency is related to the buyer's ability to obtain financing. This language is contained in almost every sales contract and is designed to protect the purchaser in the event that he or she cannot obtain the necessary financing to purchase a house. Financing contingencies generally have very short durations ranging from one week to one month and require the purchaser to take action by applying for a loan within the first 72 hours. Furthermore, the purchaser must furnish you with a copy of an approval letter once approval has been granted. Be careful with so-called pre-approval letters, because sometimes they're not worth the paper they're written on. Pre-approval letters are typically written in such a manner that they provide the lender who wrote it with all kinds of loopholes. While a pre-approval letter is an acceptable starting place for the buyer to demonstrate creditworthiness and the ability to purchase your house, what you are really looking for is a commitment letter from the lender that states in no uncertain terms that the buyer is qualified to purchase your house.

Whether or not you accept an offer with contingencies in it is entirely up to you. You should be prepared to accept an offer with a financing contingency, however, as that is a standard section contained in almost every sales agreement. The buyer must have the necessary time to obtain financing for the purchase of your house. As explained in the previous section, this should not take any longer than 30 days at the most. If the buyer wants to make the purchase of your house contingent on the sale of his house, you must consider the fact that it may take several months for his house to sell. That can put you in a holding pattern if you don't know how to properly address that particular situation. And worse yet, you could find yourself without a buyer at all if his house doesn't sell. That's not a situation you want to put yourself in. The way to protect yourself if the buyer wants to make the purchase of your house contingent on the sale of his house is by putting additional language in the contract that allows you to continue to market your house and accept offers on it. If you receive a second offer from another buyer, you are free to accept it, but the buyer who made the first offer is then given 72 hours to perform and another 30 days to close. In other words, the buyer has 72 hours to make a decision as to whether or not he or she can obtain the necessary financing to purchase your house and then close on it within the next 30 days. If the buyer can't do that, then you are under no further obligation to them and are free to accept the second offer. I use this particular strategy whenever necessary to take buyers out of the market. In other words, once they have made an offer with a sales contingency that I have accepted, they are contractually obligated to purchase my house. At the same time, I am free to sell it to another buyer should one come along in the interim. From a purely psychological perspective, I have taken the buyer out of the market because there has been a very real mental and emotional transition that has occurred for her or him. In the mind of the buyer, he or she has "purchased" a home and is therefore no longer shopping and comparing my house to those of numerous other sellers. I have effectively taken the buyer out of the market. In the meanwhile, if I can't find another buyer for my house, I still have the original buyer to fall back on when his or her house does eventually sell.

As the seller, you may be wondering if you should counter any of the buyer's contingencies. The answer to this question depends on the contingency. There are certain contingencies built into almost every sales contract that are designed to protect both parties. For example, most all purchase agreements are contingent on the buyer's ability to obtain suitable financing. If the buyer cannot do so by failing to qualify, the agreement becomes null and void and the buyer's earnest money deposit is typically refunded. On the other hand, if the buyer fails to make the effort to obtain financing within the stipulated period of time, he or she would then be considered to be in breach of contract and the earnest money would become subject to forfeiture. Another common contingency is the buyer's right to inspect the property. You may choose to give the buyer that right, but do not have to make the transaction contingent upon acceptance of the property in good condition. It can instead be sold "as is." You can also address the buyer's right to inspection by placing a cap on the amount of money you are willing to contribute to repairs. For example, if you set the cap at $1,000 and an inspector determines that the roof will need to be replaced at a cost of $4,500, your maximum exposure is only $1,000.

Another common contingency is the buyer's right to receive the property free and clear of any and all encumbrances. This means the title to the property must not have any liens, clouds, or other defects that cannot be cured placed on it. This is one contingency that you must accept because the buyer has the right to purchase your property with a clean title. Another contingency the buyer may ask for is to make the purchase of your property conditional on the sale of his or her existing residence. The advantages of this concept were discussed in the previous section. It doesn't hurt to accept an offer with this contingency in it; however, I recommend making a counteroffer that includes a provision allowing you to accept other offers until such time as the house is sold. This way you are protected in the event another buyer wants to purchase your house and has the ability to close without needing to sell his or her house.

Although there may be other contingencies that arise, the ones mentioned here are four of the most common ones. You may occasionally get something out of left field, as I did just today. I recently entered into a purchase agreement with a client to build a new home for him and his family. Apparently his lender said something today that gave him unnecessary cause for concern. The buyer wanted me to place a contingency in the contract stating that he would be entitled to a full refund of his $11,000 earnest money deposit in the event his house did not appraise for the contracted sales price once it was completed. I've never had a single incidence when a newly built house did not appraise for a minimum of its contracted selling price. I told the buyer, "Absolutely not." I explained to the buyer that I have no control over who the lender uses to do the appraisal and I wasn't about to assume the risk for something over which I have no control. Fortunately, I was able to allay the buyer's fears by reassuring him that this has never happened before. When negotiating with buyers, you must remember that the agreement must work for both of you. If the buyer includes a contingency in an offer that isn't in your best interests, then you should give serious consideration to countering it. When making a counteroffer, keep the lines of communication open with the buyer and explain in an amicable manner why you can't accept the offer as it is written. By talking it out, you may very well be able to reach a compromise that is acceptable to both of you.

Earnest Money Deposits

Earnest money is a deposit that is held in escrow by a third party such as a title company as consideration for the purchase of real estate. It can be in the form of cash, check, money order, certified funds, bank wire, or any other type of monetary form. Earnest money is given by the purchaser as security and a good faith deposit to demonstrate his or her commitment and willingness to follow through with the purchase of real estate. If a breach of contract is caused by the purchaser, the earnest money deposit is usually forfeited to the seller. Although an earnest money deposit is typically used as *consideration* to make a sales contract legally binding, most state laws do not require consideration to be in the form of money. Consideration can be anything that is of value. For example, consideration can be a tangible object such as jewelry, a car or boat, or even the family pet! Consideration can also be intangible, such as a service performed or some other type of labor. The purchaser can, for example, agree to mow your lawn, paint your house, or even do the dishes as valuable consideration for the purchase of your home!

A good rule of thumb for the amount of earnest money provided by the buyer is a minimum of 2 percent of the selling price of your house and a maximum of 5 percent. So, on a $100,000 house, the amount of earnest money should range from about $2,000 to $5,000, and on a $250,000 house, the amount of earnest money should range from about $5,000 to $12,500. This is only a general guideline and you should be prepared to be flexible with the amount of earnest money you are willing to accept. Some buyers will have no problem writing a check for the full 5 percent while others will struggle to come up with even a thousand dollars. If everything else in a buyer's purchase agreement looks good, but the amount of earnest money is a little low, I try not to let that get in the way of a sale. For example, if I know the buyers are financially qualified, they offer full asking price or close to it, and they can close when I need them to, then more than likely I will take the deal if they are a little light on the earnest money deposit.

Once you and the buyer have agreed on an acceptable amount of earnest money, the funds are then placed into an escrow account held by a third party. The buyer's earnest money check should be made payable to the third party and not you. All title companies are required to maintain escrow accounts and can act as a third party if you so choose. The funds are held in a non-interest-bearing account at no cost to the depositor. The benefit to the title company is that it will expect to generate income through title insurance services to both you and the buyer. As the seller, you must purchase an owner's policy and the buyer must purchase a mortgage policy. Some real estate attorneys also provide escrow services in conjunction with the other services they provide, such as the preparation of contracts or deeds.

What to Do When a Mutual Agreement Is Reached

When you and the buyer reach a mutual agreement, the first thing to do is make sure it is in writing. The purchase agreement should accurately reflect all that you and the buyer have discussed, including any changes that may have been made throughout the negotiation process. The topic of purchase agreements, or sales agreements, will be more fully discussed in Chapter 10. Remember that both the buyer and the seller should initial any changes as an acknowledgment of agreement with them. After the purchase agreement is completed to your satisfaction, be sure that all parties who have, or will have, a legal interest in the property sign it. This includes spouses. Although most states do not require purchase agreements to be notarized, it is nevertheless a good idea to have a witness sign it. The witness can be a friend or neighbor, or even another member of the family, and should be 18 years of age or older. Once the paperwork is completed, it's time for the buyer to give you a check for the amount of earnest money agreed upon by both of you. Recall that the earnest money deposit should be made payable to the escrow agent, which is usually the title company that will provide insurance and closing services. A copy of the purchase agreement along with the check should then be delivered to the title company. A representative will meet with you to explain the services they provide, as well as to accept the earnest money check for deposit into an escrow account. Title companies and title insurance will be more fully discussed in Chapter 11.

To summarize, communication skills are key to your success in negotiating the sale of your house. You must not only be able to recognize the telltale signs buyers provide, both verbal and nonverbal, but also know how to use them to your advantage. Buyers frequently launch trial balloons that you can use to get them to make a commitment by having them put their offers in writing. Be careful about allowing the buyer to include too many contingencies and subject to clauses as you don't want to give them too many ways to get out of a contract. Finally, be sure to collect an adequate amount of earnest money from the buyer so that you know he or she is truly committed to follow through with the purchase.

10

Formalizing the Sale: How to Use Sales Contracts and Purchase Agreements to Protect Your Legal Interests

Chapter 10 is devoted entirely to a discussion of the residential sales contract—or purchase agreement as it is also known—because this important document is an essential part of every real estate transaction. A *purchase agreement* is used to legally bind two or more parties together in contractual form to specify the terms and conditions under which real property is to be bought or sold. Sales contracts are written with many variations to cover the differing needs of the parties involved. The purchase agreement can be written in a very concise format and can be as short as one page, or it can be drafted to be much more comprehensive in nature and can be as long as 15 pages or more. Some contracts are written with simplicity in mind, while others are more carefully drafted for the purpose of protecting buyers and sellers from most any unforeseen condition that may arise. Regardless of their length or complexity, most all sales agreements have several basic components in common. Included in Appendix C, Sample Real Estate Forms, is a Residential Sales Contract you can refer to as needed.

To eliminate possible confusion, the terms *sales contract, purchase agreement*, and *sales agreement* are one and the same and are often used interchangeably. All are pledges, or covenants, used to contractually bind two or more parties to a real estate transaction. Over the years, the word *agreement* has been increasingly used to replace the word *contract* in the sale of residential property. Agreement has been used in place of contract because it has, you might say, a more agreeable connotation. Contract sounds very formal and official and suggests that a legal commitment has been made, while agreement sounds a little friendlier and more like a mutual understanding between two parties. Although a sales contract and a purchase agreement are one and the same, most buyers would prefer to sign an agreement rather than a contract. An agreement is less threatening and not as intimidating as a contract, especially to those individuals who may be first-time buyers. Keep this principle in mind as you are working with prospective buyers. You want to keep the conversation as friendly and amicable sounding as possible. The word *contract* can strike fear into the hearts of some buyers, while the word *agreement* is not nearly as threatening. Now let's take a look at the sales agreement and some of its basic components.

1. Parties

In Section 1, the seller and the buyer are identified as the parties to the contract. If there is more than one seller or buyer, the additional parties should also be named. For married couples in many states, either spouse can purchase real property without the consent of the other spouse; however, when it becomes time to sell, both spouses must be listed on the agreement. If you have any questions regarding the laws in your state, the title company you are using will be able to help you.

2. Property

Section 2 of the sales contract is used to list the property's street address and its legal description. It's important to review this section for accuracy, especially the legal description, as it is very easy to transpose the numbers. I once purchased two individual rental properties from a seller that closed on the same day. The title company got the legal addresses mixed up, and unfortunately the problem wasn't discovered until some time later when I sold them. That created additional title and legal work, which ended up being at my expense. If you don't know your property's legal description, it should be listed on a recent tax bill. You can also find it in any of the closing documents from when you originally purchased the house, or if you've refinanced it recently.

The property section is also used to identify more specifically items to be included with the purchase, such as appliances, air conditioning equipment, ceiling fans, garage door openers, and anything else the parties wish to include. *Real property* is identified as that which is generally considered to be permanent and is firmly attached to the land or property. Examples of real property include the house itself, decks and patios, sheds and pools, cabinets and countertops, and heating and air conditioning equipment. *Personal property*, on the other hand, is that property which is not permanently attached to the land or property. Examples of personal property include all of your personal effects like jewelry and clothing, furniture and wall hangings, and, of course, the kids' toys and other recreational items. There may be some items that could be categorized as either real or personal property. For example, a wooden playground structure erected in the backyard could be considered real property because it is firmly attached to the land. At the same time, it could be considered personal property because the playground equipment can be disassembled and moved to another location. Drapes and blinds are also items that can be classified in either category. Be sure to specify any items that could be considered real property if you in fact intend to take them with you. The buyer may otherwise assume they come with the house.

3. Sales Price

Section 3 is self-explanatory. It is comprised of the cash portion of the purchase price payable by the buyer, the amount of the purchase price to be financed, and the total of the two. If the price is changed during the negotiation process, be sure all parties listed on the contract initial the change.

4. Financing

The financing section in the purchase agreement provides the buyer with several different financing options. This section also sets forth the number of days the buyer has to apply for financing. Three to five days should be ample time for your buyer to begin the application process. The buyer should be prepared to have his or her lender send a form to you, commonly referred to as a prequalification letter, stating that he or she is qualified to obtain a loan up to a particular dollar amount. The amount stated in the letter should be, at a minimum, enough to purchase your house.

The third party financing section provides for mortgage or bank financing, or financing by any other third party, and also outlines the terms and conditions for the loan the buyer is seeking. There is also a provision for seller financing and loan assumptions, if needed. Finally, there is a provision to have the buyer deliver satisfactory evidence of credit to the seller if the seller financing or loan assumption provisions are used.

5. Earnest Money

The earnest money section is used to describe the deposit the buyer will provide upon acceptance of the contract by the seller. Earnest money is a form of consideration that must be furnished in any legal contract. While consideration can be anything of value that both parties agree upon, it is usually tendered in a monetary form such as a personal check, cashier's check, or money order. Sometimes a buyer may not have all of the required earnest money readily available, so will give a portion upon acceptance by the seller and provide the remainder at a later date, usually within 30 days or so. The timing for the delivery of earnest money is a negotiable item to be worked out by both the buyer and the seller. I have sold many houses on which I allow the buyer to use our "EZ payment plan." This plan allows buyers to give my company a portion of the earnest money at the time of signing, with the balance being paid over the next few weeks. I am perfectly comfortable with this arrangement and have never had a problem with the buyer's coming up with the remaining balance. If you agree to a similar arrangement, be sure to identify this in the sales contract by listing the dates and amounts for the buyer to pay the remaining balance.

6. Title Policy and Survey

The title policy is issued by a title company to assure the buyer, and more particularly the lender, that the title is free and clear of any encumbrances, or clouds, that may adversely affect the property. A cloud on a title is something that affects its marketability. If, for example, work was performed by a contractor who was not paid, even years ago, the contractor may have placed a lien on the property. The title company will perform an abstract that should reveal any such liens or clouds. The contractor's lien used in this example would have to be satisfied or resolved as a condition of closing. Otherwise, the new property owner, or buyer, would assume the previous owner's liability.

The survey, which is also covered in Section 6, is an item not to be taken lightly. Some lenders require it and some do not. The survey identifies the metes and bounds of the subject property. In other words, it identifies the exact physical location of the property. The corners or boundaries are typically set off with temporary wooden stakes and more permanent iron rods, usually about one inch in diameter and one foot long or so. The irons, as they are called, are hammered into the ground to serve as permanent markers for the property's boundaries. Chances are, the house you live in now has irons set in the ground along the perimeter of the property. If the house is even a few years old, they may be difficult to find since grass or plants and sometimes landscaping may be covering them. The problem with buyers' not getting a survey is that they may not be buying what they think they are buying.

Let's look at an example. Several years ago, my company started the construction of a new house on a lot that was adjacent to another house that had been there for about three years. We had our property physically staked by a surveying company just as we always do. When building a house from the ground up, you can't afford to take a chance on not having the lot lines and the house staked. The house could otherwise violate the setback lines required in the deed restrictions. In this particular instance, the buyer's grass and irrigation system encroached on our lot by a full fifteen feet, which was almost right up against the edge of the house we were building. The neighbor, who was apparently too cheap to get his own survey when he purchased his property, had the irrigation system and grass installed where he thought they should go. Well guess what? He was wrong. He threatened to sue us, called the city inspector out, and was downright unruly. I suppose, in a way I don't blame him, but on the other hand, it wasn't my fault that he didn't have his property surveyed. Being the good neighbors we are, and in an effort to maintain the peace, we agreed to reinstall the irrigation lines along his new property line at our expense.

As the seller, you don't have to worry about having the survey done because this is the responsibility of the buyer. Some lenders require surveys and some do not. After you sell the house you are currently living in, however, you will most likely purchase another one. Even if your lender does not require a new survey, I recommend getting one anyway so that you can be certain you are buying what you think you are buying.

7. Property Condition

Section 7 of the sales agreement outlines property inspection obligations for both the buyer and the seller. The buyer has the right to personally inspect the property for acceptable condition, as well as the right to hire a professional company to inspect it for him. At Symphony Homes, we occasionally have buyers who want their brand new homes inspected. As builders, this seems redundant to us since the house has undergone a whole series of inspections from start to finish. We don't mind, however, because the inspectors help to instill greater confidence in the consumers' minds about the quality of product we offer. The homebuyer is essentially paying for a third party impartial opinion of his or her own choosing.

In addition to a home inspection, the property condition disclosure, discussed in Chapter 5, requires the seller to fully disclose any known defects pertaining to the house. In addition, the seller must disclose any knowledge of the use of lead-based paint if the house was built before 1978. The lender may also require certain repairs if deemed necessary before agreeing to provide financing for the house. Finally, this section states that the seller must complete all required repairs prior to the date of closing unless otherwise agreed upon by both parties in writing.

8. Broker's Fees

The section on broker's fees is succinct and to the point. It basically states that the fees are provided for in a separate agreement. This section is, of course, not applicable to you because you have not engaged a real estate agent to represent you.

9. Closing

The date of closing is an essential component of all residential sales agreements. If the closing date is not met, then certain actions may be required as stipulated in the contract. In the sales contract, it states "If either party fails to close this sale by the Closing Date, the non-defaulting party will be entitled to exercise the remedies contained in Paragraph 15." Whatever sales contract you end up using, be sure that the penalties for not closing by the date specified are clearly defined. In the purchase agreements for Symphony Homes, we require buyers to pay an additional $100 per day for every day the date of closing is delayed beyond a seven-day grace period. Our contracts did not contain the penalty clause in them initially. However, as a result of buyers who found a myriad of creative ways to delay the closing because they had not yet sold their houses, the language was added as a protective measure. This may sound a bit severe to some readers, but from our perspective, the penalty serves two important functions. First, it signals to the buyer that we are serious about closing on time and that failure to do so will result in a substantial penalty, and second, the penalty helps to offset our carrying costs, which include interest, taxes, insurance, utilities, and the loss of use of the company's capital. In summary, consider your specific needs as they relate to the closing and make sure they are included in the sales contract.

10. Possession

Section 10 of the agreement pertains to the date possession is given to the buyer. The date of possession is usually, but not always, the date of the closing. Circumstances may arise that prevent the granting of possession until a later date. You should also be aware when granting possession that it should not be given only at the time of closing. In our contracts, we specify that the date of possession is granted "upon closing and *funding*." This means that not only does all of the paperwork have to be completed with all of the appropriate signatures, but also that the buyer's loan must fund. In other words, the title company managing the closing for us must be prepared to wire funds to our account at the time of closing. If a closing is scheduled for a Friday, be careful that it is not too late in the day. If, for example, it is at 4:00 PM and all of the documents are not signed until 5:00 or after, the deal will probably not fund until the following Monday. What happens is that as soon as all of the documents are signed and all conditions have been met, the title company's agent, or closer, must call the lender to get a funding number before issuing a check or wiring funds. Without that number, they will not release the funds. Guess where everybody is, including the lender's mortgage department, at 5:00 PM on Friday afternoon? That's right! They're gone for the weekend! That means the loan will not fund until the following Monday.

If the loan doesn't fund until Monday, that means you don't get any money until Monday. As far as you're concerned, you've sold your house but don't have anything to show for it, at least not yet. So now what? The buyer has done her part, but you haven't received your money. I can assure you that in most instances you will be under extreme pressure to hand over the keys to an anxious buyer who already has a moving service lined up, along with friends and family, to help with a move that is scheduled for that weekend. As far as the buyer is concerned, she has done her part. She has obtained a loan and signed all of the documents. It isn't her fault the lender hasn't authorized the release of the funds. As the seller, this places you in a very difficult position. Do you hand over the keys to accommodate them, or do you stand firm until you get your money? If you let the buyers move in over the weekend, they now have possession of the property and are no longer motivated to see that you receive your funds. If, for some reason, one of the conditions of closing had not been met, the lender who was gone over the weekend may be reluctant to fund the loan. On the other hand, if you don't allow the buyers to move in, their entire scheduling will be thrown off and they will no doubt be very upset. The buyers will, however, be highly motivated to contact the lender first thing Monday morning to find out when the loan is going to fund. The best answer is to avoid this situation all together by scheduling the closing early enough on Friday, or even a day earlier in the week, so that you don't put yourself in that position to begin with.

11. Special Provisions

This section allows both parties to write in anything that falls outside of the standard provisions already embodied within the sales agreement. For example, language addressing special needs such a contingency or subject-to clause may be included here. The Special Provisions section can be used for just about anything you want to state or otherwise clarify a specific point.

12. Settlement and Other Expenses

Settlement charges vary from area to area and state to state. What may be considered buyer's settlement charges in one area may be seller's charges in another area. In general, the buyer pays for an appraisal if required by his or her lender. The buyer also typically pays for any charges associated with a new loan. This includes points, underwriting fees, application fees, recording fees, and other miscellaneous fees, such as the preparation of the deed. Some states require that a transfer tax be paid at the time of sale. Michigan is one of them. Unless otherwise stipulated in the contract, the seller is required to pay the tax. In summary, what may be reasonable and customary charges for buyers and sellers in one area may not be in another area.

13. Prorations

This section simply states that costs or expenses associated with the property shall be *prorated*, or apportioned, as of the date of the transfer, which is usually the date of closing. Items that are typically prorated include taxes, association fees, maintenance fees, rental income, and any other income or expenses related to the property. To prorate means to apportion or to assign the expense or income to the party entitled to it based upon the date of ownership. Let's look at an example. If the seller prepaid $3,000 in taxes for the current year beginning January 1 and the closing occurred on June 30, then the seller would be entitled to receive a credit at closing as follows:

$$(\$3,000/365) \times (365 - 181) =$$
$$\$8.21917 \times 184 = \$1,512.33$$

In this example, because the seller has prepaid the taxes in advance for the current year, she would be entitled to receive a credit on the day of closing for the remaining balance of the tax that has already been paid at a rate of roughly $8.22 per diem, or per day. The per diem rate is then multiplied by the number of days prepaid to calculate the credit due her.

14. Casualty Loss

This section provides for unforeseen property damage due to what is referred to as a *casualty loss*. It essentially covers damage to the property resulting from acts of nature such as wind, rain, or ice, as well as damage from fire. In the event the property suffers some type of damage, it becomes incumbent upon the seller to repair the damage by the date of closing, or a date at some time beyond the date of closing, provided that both parties agree. If the seller cannot repair the property in a timely manner that is satisfactory to the buyer, the buyer then has the right to terminate his interest in the contract and is entitled to a refund of his or her earnest money deposit.

15. Default

Default provisions specify what actions are to be taken in the event either party defaults on the contract. Both parties generally have the right to enforce performance of the defaulting party by seeking legal redress or extending the time or date of the contract to allow for performance. If the buyer is in default and cannot cure, depending on the circumstances, the seller will be entitled to keep the earnest money as liquidated damages. If the seller is in default, the buyer will be entitled to a refund of the earnest money.

16. Dispute Resolution

Rather than attempt to resolve disagreements through the courts, provisions are often established to encourage the use of a more peaceful solution, such as an impartial third party mediator. Although representation by an attorney may be advised, it is generally quicker and less costly if a solution can be reached outside of the court system.

17. Attorney's Fees

Section 17 simply states that in the event an agreement cannot be reached through arbitration, then the prevailing party will be entitled to a reimbursement of all legal and court costs.

18. Escrow

The parties in real estate transactions use an escrow account to deposit earnest money into. An escrow agent is used to protect the interests of both buyer and seller. Since the buyer putting up the earnest money deposit does not want to give it directly to the seller, the money is usually given to an escrow agent to hold in an escrow account. If a dispute arises, the party not in default is entitled to the earnest money. The escrow agent, however, must have a signature by both parties agreeing to the release of funds to the non-defaulting party. Most of the time, this requirement does not present a problem. If, however, the buyer defaults and does not purchase the house for a reason he or she believes is justified, and the seller seeks to receive the earnest money as liquidated damages, the buyer may refuse to sign the escrow agent's release. Failure to do so will force the parties into either arbitration or the courts.

19. Representations

Section 19 provides for the seller's representations that "there will be no liens, assessments, or security interests against the property which will not be satisfied out of the sales proceeds." In other words, this section helps to ensure that all debts against the property made by the seller will be satisfied at the time of closing and will not be carried forward to the new property owner, or buyer. Although the title company can determine if there are any liens existing against the property at the time the abstract is pulled, this does not guarantee that a party who has not been paid for services performed at the property cannot place a lien against it at a later date. For example, if a seller spent $5,000 on a new roof just before selling the house and failed to pay the contractor who provided the services, the contractor may still have the right to place a lien on the property even after it has been sold. This places the buyer in the position of having a lien against the property for which he or she is not responsible. Section 19 is designed to protect the buyer in situations like this by expressly stating that the seller has the obligation to satisfy all such debts against the property either prior to, or at the time of, the closing. In the event that the seller fails to satisfy all such debts, then the buyer is protected and can seek legal redress in the courts if necessary.

20. Federal Tax Requirement

This section provides for the collection of taxes by the Internal Revenue Service for sellers who are deemed to be "foreign persons" as defined by applicable law.

21. Agreement of Parties

Section 21 contains a very brief provision that simply states that the contract embodies the entire agreement and no other contracts will have any effect on this agreement except for any addenda which may be attached.

22. Consult Your Attorney

This section is self-explanatory and states that real estate agents cannot give legal advice and that if the parties to the contract have any questions regarding the interpretation of the agreement, then they should seek the advice of an attorney before signing the document. If you choose not to use an attorney, then it is of course up to you to ensure that the agreement is properly completed.

In summary, a purchase agreement, or sales contract, is a legally binding document used for the transfer of real property between two or more parties. It can be as short and concise as one page, or as long and comprehensive as 15 or more pages. The sample contract used in this chapter is fairly exhaustive and addresses almost all aspects that arise in a typical sale. For those items falling outside of the scope of this agreement, Section 11 has been provided to allow for the inclusion of any special provisions. You may also want to check with your title company to determine whether or not any issues specific to your state need to be included in the contract.

PART III

The FSBO's
Closing Checklist

11

Title Insurance: How to Select the Best Title Company and Have the Buyer Pay for It

Title companies are an essential part of real property sales transactions, especially for the FSBO. A title company can assist both the buyer and seller by providing key services, including maintaining escrow deposits, providing a title report and title insurance, and managing the closing process. While most title companies offer similar services, they vary greatly in the degree to which they can provide those services. Furthermore, the fees title companies charge for services can also vary widely. This chapter is intended to educate you about title companies and the services they offer, alert you to some of the pitfalls to be aware of when working with a title company, help you to identify a competent title company in your area, and, finally, learn how to have the buyer pay for all or part of the services.

The Necessity of Title Services

A *title* refers to the rights and usage of ownership and possession of property, whether personal or real. An example of a commonly used title for personal property is the title to the vehicle you drive. Regardless of whether you drive a car, a motorcycle, a boat, or a snowmobile to work each day, a title was issued with the vehicle at the time of purchase. With real property, title may refer to the instruments or documents by which a right of ownership is established (title documents), or it may refer to the ownership interest one has in the real estate. Title to real property is typically issued in the form of a *deed*. Recall from Chapter 5 that a deed is a formal written instrument by which title to real property is transferred from one owner to another. The deed should contain an accurate description of the property being conveyed, should be signed and witnessed according to the laws of the state where the property is located, and should be delivered to the purchaser on the day of closing.

A title search, also known as the abstract of title, is performed to check the history of the title records to ensure that the buyer is purchasing a house from the legal owner and also to be certain that there are no liens, overdue special assessments, unpaid taxes, unpaid water and sewer charges, or other claims or outstanding restrictive covenants filed in the record that would have an unfavorable impact on the marketability or value of a property's title. In other words, the title report shows the property's chain of title by listing a history of ownership, as well as judgments, liens, and anything else that may have been recorded against the property over time. The title insurance company issues an insurance policy to the buyer and a separate policy to the lender that ensures the title is clean and free of encumbrances. In addition, title insurance protects lenders or homeowners against loss of their interest in property due to legal defects in the title that may remain undiscovered until some time after the closing has occurred. Title insurance may be issued to a mortgagee's title policy. Insurance benefits will be paid only to the "named insured" in the title policy, so it is important that an owner purchase an "owner's title policy" for protection against loss from any such defects.

All Title Companies Are Not Created Equal

In general, although the majority of title companies provide a full range of title services, they vary widely in the quality of service offered. I've worked with many companies over the years and each one seems to have its quirks. While some of these peculiarities are fairly minor in the grand scheme of things, others are quite significant. For example, one title company I used to do business with several years ago had a rather pathetic operations department. My contact there was the company's outside salesman, who himself understood the importance of being customer focused. Although he did an outstanding job of addressing my needs, the company's back office, which is where the title work is processed, had no clue regarding what it meant to be customer focused. I sent the title company seven or eight deals shortly after switching my business to them and ended up having problems with almost every one of them. I had problems with scheduled closings that had previously been confirmed for a particular date and then mysteriously disappeared from their appointment book. I had problems with the firm's people in operations, who were supposedly able to prepare all of the title work, but just couldn't seem to get it right. And, finally, I had problems with their closing officers who also proved themselves to be incapable. Although the sales rep did everything he could to help me, the rest of the people there just didn't seem to get it.

Now that I've lamented over my unfavorable experience with this title company, let me conclude on a more positive note. The title company that I am currently using is run the way a title company is supposed to be run. For the most part, I can send them a deal and schedule a closing for just about any time I need it. Their operations department is among the best I've seen when it comes to things running smoothly and efficiently. I don't have to be concerned about the quality of title work from them, knowing that the company goes the extra mile to ensure accuracy. Finally, the closing officer I work with provides excellent service and closes at my office at the convenience of my company and its clients.

How to Find a Superior Title Company in Your Area

While many buyers and sellers have no preference regarding which title company is to be used, in most states, it is the seller who has the right to select the title company. As a FSBO, it is a good idea to do your homework in advance and begin looking for a competent title company. Unless you're in the business of buying and selling real estate on a regular basis, chances are you may not know of a good title company that can provide quality services in your area. Just because the company may conduct business at a national level and be recognized nationwide doesn't mean that particular office can provide you with the level of service you deserve. I've observed over the years that service and competency come down to individual offices and the people who run them. Key factors to look for center around competitive fees, excellent service, and quality title work. By calling several title companies, you can shop and compare title fees just like you can shop and compare anything else.

To assess the type of service you might expect, I recommend observing the general demeanor of the people at the office. Are they professional and polite, or do they treat you like they don't have time for you? Can they schedule you for a closing when you need it, and can they schedule you for a closing on short notice if needed, or do they require a minimum of two to three weeks advance notice to get you in? Evaluating the quality of the operations department is not as easy to do for the individual who has only an occasional real estate transaction. To find a competent title company in your area, I recommend asking some of the local real estate agents who deal with them on a routine basis. This can be done in the initial stages when you are gathering information, such as comparative market analysis studies, in preparation for selling your house. Simply ask the agents what title company they prefer doing business with and why they like using them. Be sure to ask them also about things like scheduling a closing, the level of service provided, whether or not the services are competitively priced, and if they have experienced any problems with the title company.

How to Get the Buyer to Pay for Title Insurance

Most standard purchase agreements stipulate that the buyer is responsible for paying for the lender's title policy and that the seller is responsible for paying for the owner's title policy. Logically speaking, this makes perfect sense since the buyer is insuring the lender against loss and the seller is insuring the new owner against loss. As a homeowner selling your own house, you will in all likelihood provide the buyer with a purchase agreement when the time comes to sign the contract. If you are using your own forms, getting the buyer to pay for what is typically deemed a seller expense is as easy as changing the word *seller* to the word *buyer* in the section that covers title insurance. If you have the sales agreement in a word processor format, this is very easy to do. When it comes time to fill out the agreement with the buyer, review this section with him or her just as you would the rest of the contract. Unless the buyer is active in the real estate market, he or she is not even likely to know the difference, especially if it is written into the contract that way. Remember that almost all closing costs are negotiable anyway, so you are certainly not doing anything illegal by requiring the buyer to pay for the owner's policy. My own personal contracts are drafted this way, and occasionally a buyer will ask about it, but more often than not, we cover the point and keep right on moving through the agreement. There is no trickery involved and no pulling the wool over anyone's eyes. If the buyer wants to object, he or she has the right to do so before signing the agreement.

Title Company Fees

Title companies, like any other companies, are in business to earn a profit. Although most of their revenues are generated by selling title insurance, a substantial portion of their revenue is derived through various fees. While the rate charged for insurance is often mandated by statute, the fees charged by title companies can vary widely depending on the area you are in, so it pays to shop around. Table 11.1 provides a list of fees commonly charged by title companies and a general price range for them.

The closing fee is paid to the title company for doing the actual closing. This includes the preparation of all the necessary documents, which can be quite involved. This is especially true of the buyer's side of the transaction because of all of the seemingly endless forms lenders require them to sign. Recording fees are charged to reimburse the title company for recording the various legal documents at the county courthouse. Oftentimes, overnight fees are charged to reimburse the title company for documents that are mailed by the lender with overnight service. With the

Table 11.1

Type of Fee	Low	High
Closing	$100.00	$500.00
Recording	$10.00	$45.00
Overnight	$20.00	$40.00
Document Preparation	$50.00	$300.00
Administrative	$25.00	$100.00

ability to send entire loan packages to the title company via e-mail, however, overnight fees are becoming less common.

When to Order Your Title Work

If you've owned your house for several years and haven't had any issues arise that are related to its title, then it's fairly safe to wait until you have a buyer and the house is placed under contract before submitting it to the title company to have an abstract run. On the other hand, if you are aware of any unresolved disputes that may have caused a lien or judgment to be placed on your house, then it is a good idea to go ahead and order the title work when you first place the house on the market for sale. One example of an unresolved dispute is a contractor who wasn't paid for work performed. Not only can the contractor who did the work place a lien against your house, but the vendor who supplied him with the materials can as well. Even if you've paid the contractor in full, the suppliers furnishing the materials to the contractor still have the right to place a lien on your property if they are not paid by the contractor. As unfair as this may seem, suppliers have the right to take specific measures as prescribed by law to issue a notice of furnishment. If the contractor performing the labor fails to pay for the materials, the supplier has the right to attach a lien to the property on which the materials were used. I've experienced this very issue from time to time with the many contractors who work for my company. For example, I once had a painter who was paid in full for services rendered, but who in turn failed to pay his account with a national paint supply company. The paint supplier in turn placed liens against not one, but three, of my properties until the matter was resolved.

Another example of an unresolved dispute or obligation is homeowner association dues that may not have been paid for any number of reasons. Perhaps the association had what seemed like an unjustified increase in the annual dues, and many of the residents there refused to pay them. Homeowner's associations do have the right to attach liens to property for any unpaid dues, knowing that they will eventually have to be paid in order for the homeowner to sell his or her house. Interest and penalties may also be included in the charges. If you're not aware of any disputes or unresolved issues, there's a good chance there are none. So the time to submit your order to the title company for an abstract, or title search, is when you have the property under contract with a buyer.

Title Searches: How Long Do They Take?

The time required to do a title search can be as little as a couple of days, and as long as a couple of months or more. The average title search, however, takes just a few days to complete. This will vary by area, by company, and by economic conditions. For example, during the refinance boom when practically everyone got a new mortgage because of historically low rates, getting the title work done in some areas could easily take several weeks. In a more stable economic environment, however, if the title is clear and there are no encumbrances affecting it, then a title search can be done in as little as a few days. On the other hand, if the title is clouded with a lien, or perhaps the chain of title is unclear, then it could take several days, or even several weeks, to resolve. If there is a dispute with a tax authority, for example, on the amount of taxes owed, it could take a month or two, or even more, to get the matter worked out. If you're in a hurry to sell and the tax authority demands payment, you may have no choice but to pay the additional taxes because you won't be able to transfer the title until you do. I once had a buyer who just happened to own a title company. She came out to look at one of our spec houses that was ready for immediate occupancy on a Monday and made an offer on it the very next day. I accepted her offer on Wednesday, and we scheduled the closing for the next Monday. So from start to finish, my client picked out a house, did the title work, had her financing ready, and closed on it all within one week!

In summary, finding and using a competent title company is essential to selling your house successfully. Recall that a title company can assist buyers and sellers by providing important services necessary to transfer real property from one party to another. These include holding the earnest money deposit in an escrow account, performing abstracts, providing title insurance, and offering closing services. And just like any other product or service you spend your hard-earned money on, it pays to shop around to find a title company that is capable of handling your needs at competitive rates.

12

Home Inspections: How to Comply with the Home Inspection Process

Although in theory a home inspection may be something sellers dread, in practice it can actually serve as a measure by which they can be protected against future lawsuits. In this chapter, we'll discuss the right of the buyer to have an inspection done; how to minimize the time frame allowed for the inspection; what steps you can take to protect yourself against litigation, whether an inspection is done or not; the inspection process itself; and how to minimize your out-of-pocket expenses for items that are found to be defective, faulty, or just plain worn out.

The Buyer's Right to Inspect

The first question that arises is, "Do I have to let the buyer inspect my house?" The answer to that question depends on how badly you want to sell it. If you are unwilling to allow the buyer to inspect your house, he or she may believe you have something to hide. Put yourself in the buyer's place for a moment. Would you purchase something valued at $100,000 or $200,000 without being able to look it over and make sure that everything worked properly? My guess is, probably not. The buyer of your house is no different. While buyers do have the right to have an inspection done, they are responsible for bearing the cost. After all, it is the buyer who is requesting the inspection—not you.

Although some buyers may feel comfortable doing the inspection themselves, others will want to hire a professional inspector. Rather than resist an inspection, you should welcome the request to have one done. This will signal to the buyer that you have confidence in the condition and functionality of your house and that you have nothing to hide. And who knows? Your manifestation of confidence in the condition of your house may just make the buyer feel comfortable enough to accept it without having an inspection done. One reason for this is that by not having an inspection done, the buyer will save $250 to $500. For buyers who are on a tight budget, the cost of an inspection is reason enough not to have one done.

How to Minimize the Time Frame Allowed for the Inspection

The time to stipulate the conditions by which an inspection will be performed is when the purchase agreement is drafted. Your purchase agreement should have a provision within it that covers the inspection process. The provision should cover who pays for the inspection, when it will be completed, and what steps are to be taken as a result of the findings. If the buyer requests that an inspection be done on your house, then I suggest that you respond by saying something like, "Mrs. Buyer, I'll be happy to let you hire the inspector of your choice; however, if you're going to have one done, I'd like to get that out of the way first thing. Do you think two weeks will allow you enough time?" Your willingness to allow the buyer to have an inspection done will, in and of itself, be reassuring to her. If the buyer says she needs more time, I recommend giving her no more than three weeks. In most areas, it only takes a day or two to schedule a professional home inspector and, depending on how busy the company is, it shouldn't take any longer than two to three weeks at the outside for it to complete the report.

It's important for you, as the seller, to keep this inspection window as small as possible to minimize the time your house is off the market. You don't want the buyers to tie up your property indefinitely, for example, by granting them the right to hold off on the inspection until a few days before the closing. Doing so will give them a legal out if the inspector finds something that needs repairing. In the final days before the closing, the buyers could demand that you lower the price, give them a credit to cover the cost of the repair, have the item fixed, or simply walk away. By specifying in the purchase agreement that the inspection must be completed no later than two to three weeks after signing it, you are minimizing the risk that such an event will occur.

Although your property is under contract and, for all practical purposes, considered to be sold, you can continue showing your house to potential buyers, and even take backup offers, during the period of time allowed for the inspection. I recommend making this very clear to the current buyers by telling them that because their offer is contingent upon acceptance of the house after an inspection is done, you must continue to show it and will even entertain backup offers. This way, after the inspection has been completed, if the buyer rejects your house based on the findings in the report, you haven't lost valuable time by taking it off of the market altogether. Informing the buyers of your intent to continue showing the house may also serve to reinforce in their minds that you are serious about getting your house sold, with or without their help.

Three Steps You Can Take to Protect Yourself from Being Sued

Regardless of whether or not the buyer has your house inspected, you can protect yourself against future litigation. That's right. It doesn't matter if the buyer has your house inspected or not—that is, if you take the proper precautions. You can protect yourself by including language in the purchase agreement that protects you whether the buyer has the house inspected or not. For example, if the buyer chooses to have the house inspected and that right is granted within the contract, then the buyer has been made fully aware of the physical condition of your house as reflected in the inspection report. If there is anything wrong with the house, then it should be in the report. If a condition shows up at some point in the future, you cannot be held responsible for it because there was no evidence of it at the time the inspection was completed.

A second step you can take to protect yourself is to let the buyer choose the company that will perform the inspection. This way, you can't be accused of using someone who may have been biased because you knew them. If the buyer selected the inspection company and the company didn't find anything wrong with your house, how can you possibly be held liable for a problem detected after the sale? After all, if a professional inspector couldn't find anything wrong with the house, how could the courts possibly expect the seller to be aware of a defect? The answer is, they can't.

Finally, if the buyer chooses not to inspect your house, you can still protect yourself against a lawsuit regarding defects that might arise after the sale. Once again, the place where you can protect yourself is in the purchase agreement. If the buyer elects not to have an inspection done, this can be reflected in the contract by stating that the buyer is waiving his or her right to have an inspection done and is willing to accept the house "as is." Whether a problem is detected before the sale or after the sale, the buyer has already stated in the contract that she is willing to accept the property in its current condition. Moreover, because the buyer has waived the right to inspect the property, you cannot be held liable for any defects before or after the sale. Whether or not the buyer has your house inspected, the most important aspect of protecting yourself is to spell it out in writing at the time the contract is entered into.

What to Expect During the Inspection

You will generally need to allow at least a couple of hours for the inspector to complete a thorough examination of your house, so be sure to set aside plenty of time. The buyer may also want to tag along to see firsthand what the inspector finds, which you should gladly allow. Remember, you don't have anything to hide, so by giving the buyer and inspector liberal access to your house, you are sending a nonverbal signal that expresses confidence in its condition. When the big day finally arrives, the inspector will most likely show up with the standard tools of the trade. These include a pen or pencil, a clipboard with the appropriate forms attached to it, a flashlight, and a device called a voltmeter that is used to test electrical outlets. The inspector will then examine each room of the house by testing light switches, electrical outlets, appliances, heating and ventilation equipment, faucets and fixtures, the water heater and all plumbing equipment, as well as the electrical panel box. He will also examine the general condition of flooring, painting, and walls. If the house has a basement, the inspector will examine its walls for cracks and any evidence of leaks, as well as for signs of mold. In addition to examining the interior of the house and its basement, he will also need access to the attic to look for evidence of leakage, existence and condition of insulation, and any equipment that may be in the attic.

After completing an examination of the interior of your house, the inspector will then begin to look at the outside. He will inspect the exterior walls, the windows, porches, and, finally, the roof. The inspector looks not only at the functionality of an item, but also its general age and condition. For example, the inspector may note the fact that, while the roof is doing its job now, its remaining useful life is estimated to be no more than three years. Once the report is completed, the inspector will review it with you and the buyer and discuss those items that are in the most need of repair, if any. Be sure to ask for a copy of the report for your records as well. This way if the buyer mentions a problem with the house, you have the same report he or she has that you can now refer to.

How to Minimize Your Out-of-Pocket Expenses

The best way to minimize your out-of-pocket expenses is by specifying in the sales contract the dollar amount of repairs that you are willing to be responsible for. For example, assume that, after the inspection has been completed, the report states that a total of $4,500 in repairs is needed. If you and the buyer have already agreed in the contract at the time of signing that you would be responsible for no more than $2,500 in repairs, then you are not obligated for the remaining $2,000 for repairs the inspector says are needed. There is a trade-off, however. If the buyer's willingness to purchase your house is contingent upon the inspection, she may not want to go through with the purchase knowing that additional repairs are required. If this is the case, then you have three choices. First, you can stand firm on the $2,500 already agreed to, but you run the risk of losing the buyer. Second, you can agree to pay for the additional $2,000 in repairs, but doing so will cost you $2,000 that you have not agreed to. Finally, you can attempt to negotiate with the buyer to get them to pay, for example, for half of the additional repairs. Before committing one way or another, I suggest feeling the buyer out to see what she is willing to do. For example, if the buyer has been excited and very enthusiastic about the house all along, then there's a good chance she is going to be willing to pay the additional repair money, thereby allowing you to stand firm on the previously agreed upon amount of $2,500. On the other hand, if the buyer seems to be looking for an excuse not to purchase your house, then start by trying to get her to pay for half of the additional repairs, and, if that doesn't work, then you may end up paying for them yourself. The other option, of course, is to let the buyer walk away and put your house back on the market. You must weigh the strength of the market in your area and how long it will take to get another buyer under contract in making your decision. Even if you let the buyer walk away, there's a good chance that the next buyer will want the repairs completed, too, so it may make sense to go ahead and concede with the current buyer by making the needed repairs.

In summary, while the inspection process itself is fairly straightforward, it is the inspector's findings that have the potential to delay the sale. If the inspector finds a problem area, for example, the buyer may insist that it be repaired prior to the closing. Remember though, that while the inspection may be something you initially dread, it can actually save you money in the long run by protecting you against the possibility of being held liable for something that is discovered to be faulty at a later date. The best way to do this is by specifying your and the buyer's responsibilities at the time the purchase agreement is first prepared.

13

How to Understand and Comply with Appraisal Requirements

Recall from Chapter 4 that an appraisal is an estimate of an object's worth or value, and it can be used to determine the value of both personal property and real property. Recall also the statement by author William N. Kinnard in *Income Property Valuation* as it relates to the appraisal process of real property.

> An appraisal is a professionally derived conclusion about the present worth or value of specified rights or interests in a particular parcel of real estate under stipulated market conditions or decision standards. Moreover, it is (or should be) based on the professional judgment and skill of a trained practitioner. Its conclusions should be presented in a thoroughly logical and convincing way to a client or an interested third party who requires the value estimate to help make a decision or solve a problem involving the real estate in question.

Understanding Appraisals

Appraisers use one or more of the three primary methods of appraising real property. They are the *income capitalization* method, the *replacement cost* method, and the *sales comparison* method. The income capitalization method is used to determine the value of income-producing properties such as multifamily apartments or commercial buildings. Its value is derived primarily as a function of the income and resulting net yield produced by the property. This method is not used for appraising residential real estate. The replacement cost method, or *cost approach* as it is also known, is used to estimate the cost of replacing physical assets in today's dollars with adjustments made for the remaining useful life of the asset. While this method can be used to appraise residential property, it is generally used only for insurance purposes and is not intended to derive a value to be used for resale.

The third method of appraising real property is the sales comparison method, and it is the most commonly used method of appraising residential property. The sales comparison method is based upon the premise of *substitution* and maintains that a buyer would not pay any more for real property than the cost of purchasing an equally desirable substitute in its respective market. This approach also assumes that all comparable sales used in the appraisal process are legitimate arm's length transactions. The sales comparison method furthermore provides that comparable sales used have occurred under normal market conditions. For example, this assumption would exclude properties bought and sold under foreclosure conditions, or those purchased from a bank's real estate owned, or REO, portfolio. Once these properties are fixed and prepared for resale, however, the sales comparison method would then be the most appropriate method to use. Recall from Chapter 4 the discussion about doing a comparative market analysis, or CMA, to estimate the value of your house. Appraisers use a similar approach, comparing and contrasting like properties, but with a much higher degree of objectivity. In other words, the appraiser follows a set of guidelines to help estimate value. Although the guidelines do not eliminate the subjective nature of the valuation process, they do help appraisers form a professional opinion by providing uniform standards to estimate value. (See Figure 13.1.)

How to Understand and Comply with Appraisal Requirements

Figure 13.1

Lapeer Appraisal, Inc.

UNIFORM RESIDENTIAL APPRAISAL REPORT

Property Description   File No. 0515212

Property Address 827 Gardenia	City Davison State MI Zip Code 48423

Legal Description Lot 33, Laurel Heights Condo, City of Davison, Genesee County, Michigan   County Genesee

Assessor's Parcel No. 25-52-03-676-033   Tax Year ------- R.E. Taxes $ 0.00   Special Assessments $ 0.00

Borrower   Current Owner Symphony Homes, LLC   Occupant: ☐ Owner ☐ Tenant ☒ Vacant

Property rights appraised ☒ Fee Simple ☐ Leasehold   Project Type ☐ PUD ☒ Condominium (HUD/VA only)   HOA$ 8.33 /Mo.

Neighborhood or Project Name Laurel Heights, City of Davison   Map Reference GeoCode   Census Tract 049 0117.10

Sale Price $ 166,965   Date of Sale pending   Description and $ amount of loan charges/concessions to be paid by seller N/A

Lender/Client Flagstar Bank, FSB   Address 5151 Corporate Drive, Troy, MI 48098

Appraiser Dale R. Hager   Address 208 E. Genesee Street, Lapeer, MI 48446

Location	☒ Urban ☐ Suburban ☐ Rural	Predominant occupancy	Single family housing	Present land use %	Land use change
Built up	☒ Over 75% ☐ 25-75% ☐ Under 25%		PRICE $(000) AGE (yrs)	One family 90%	☒ Not likely ☐ Likely
Growth rate	☐ Rapid ☒ Stable ☐ Slow	☒ Owner	80 Low new	2-4 family	☐ In process
Property values	☐ Increasing ☒ Stable ☐ Declining	☐ Tenant	220 High 100+	Multi-family	To:
Demand/supply	☐ Shortage ☒ In balance ☐ Over supply	☒ Vacant (0-5%)	Predominant	Commercial	
Marketing time	☐ Under 3 mos. ☒ 3-6 mos. ☐ Over 6 mos.	☐ Vacant (over 5%)	140 25	Vacant 10%	

Note: Race and the racial composition of the neighborhood are not appraisal factors.

Neighborhood boundaries and characteristics: The neighborhood consists of the City of Davison

Factors that affect the marketability of the properties in the neighborhood (proximity to employment and amenities, employment stability, appeal to market, etc.): This is a neighborhood of single family dwellings located in the City of Davison. Schools and all typical amenities are provided in Davison. The employment stability appears to be average.

Market conditions in the subject neighborhood (including support for the above conclusions related to the trend of property values, demand/supply, and marketing time - - such as data on competitive properties for sale in the neighborhood, description of the prevalence of sales and financing concessions, etc.): Sales prices indicate that values are stable to slightly increasing. Typical marketing time is 3-6 months and few financing concessions are required. Financing is readily available from a variety of sources.

Project Information for PUDs (If applicable) - - Is the developer/builder in control of the Home Owners' Association (HOA)? ☐ YES ☐ NO

Approximate total number of units in the subject project _____ . Approximate total number of units for sale in the subject project _____

Describe common elements and recreational facilities:

Dimensions irregular		Topography nearly level
Site area .18 Acres +/-	Corner Lot ☐ Yes ☒ No	Size typical
Specific zoning classification and description A-3 Residential District		Shape slightly irregular
Zoning compliance ☒ Legal ☐ Legal nonconforming (Grandfathered use) ☐ Illegal ☐ No zoning		Drainage appears adequate
Highest & best use as improved: ☒ Present use ☐ Other use (explain)		View neighborhood

Utilities	Public	Other	Off-site Improvements	Type	Public	Private	
Electricity	☒		Street	paved	☒	☐	Landscaping none
Gas	☒		Curb/gutter	yes	☒	☐	Driveway Surface paved
Water	☒		Sidewalk	yes	☒	☐	Apparent easements public utilities
Sanitary sewer	☒		Street lights	yes	☒	☐	FEMA Special Flood Hazard Area ☐ Yes ☒ No
Storm sewer	☒		Alley	none	☐	☐	FEMA Zone Zone C Map Date 6/15/79
							FEMA Map No. 2606640005 B

Comments (apparent adverse easements, encroachments, special assessments, slide areas, illegal or legal nonconforming zoning, use, etc.): No easements, encroachments, or other adverse conditions were apparent other than those for public utilities.

GENERAL DESCRIPTION	EXTERIOR DESCRIPTION	FOUNDATION	BASEMENT	INSULATION
No. of Units 1	Foundation conc block	Slab	Area Sq.Ft. 630	Roof ☐
No. of Stories 2	Exterior Walls vinyl	Crawl Space	% Finished 0%	Ceiling ☒
Type (Det./Att.) detached	Roof Surface asph shingles	Basement full	Ceiling	Walls ☒
Design (Style) 2 story	Gutters & Dwnspts. yes	Sump Pump yes	Walls	Floor ☐
Existing/Proposed proposed	Window Type vinyl	Dampness not apparent	Floor	None ☐
Age (Yrs.) new	Storm/Screens thermal/yes	Settlement not apparent	Outside Entry	Unknown ☐
Effective Age (Yrs.) 0	Manufactured House no	Infestation not apparent		

ROOMS	Foyer	Living	Dining	Kitchen	Den	Family Rm.	Rec. Rm.	Bedrooms	# Baths	Laundry	Other	Area Sq.Ft.
Basement												630
Level 1	1		1	1		1			.5			630
Level 2								3	2	1		779

Finished area **above grade** contains: 6 Rooms; 3 Bedroom(s); 2.5 Bath(s); 1,409 Square Feet of Gross Living Area

INTERIOR	Materials/Condition	HEATING		KITCHEN EQUIP.		ATTIC		AMENITIES		CAR STORAGE:	
Floors	carpet/vinyl	Type	FA	Refrigerator	☐	None	☐	Fireplace(s) #0	☐	None	☐
Walls	drywall	Fuel	NG	Range/Oven	☐	Stairs	☐	Patio none	☐	Garage	# of cars
Trim/Finish	wood/painted	Condition	good	Disposal	☐	Drop Stair	☐	Deck none	☐	Attached	2
Bath Floor	vinyl	COOLING		Dishwasher	☒	Scuttle	☒	Porch covered	☒	Detached	
Bath Wainscot	none	Central	yes	Fan/Hood	☐	Floor	☐	Fence none	☐	Built-In	
Doors	masonite panel	Other	none	Microwave	☐	Heated	☐	Pool none	☐	Carport	
		Condition		Washer/Dryer	☐	Finished	☐			Driveway	

Additional features (special energy efficient items, etc.):

Condition of the improvements, depreciation (physical, functional, and external), repairs needed, quality of construction remodeling/additions, etc.: The condition of the improvements is good and the quality of construction is average. Depreciation is typical for a house of this age. The condition of the furnace was determined by visual inspection only.

Adverse environmental conditions (such as, but not limited to, hazardous wastes, toxic substances, etc.) present in the improvements, on the site, or in the immediate vicinity of the subject property: No adverse environmental conditions were apparent to the appraiser. See Addendum

Freddie Mac Form 70 6-93   PAGE 1 OF 2   Produced using ACI software, 800.234.8727 www.aciweb.com   Fannie Mae Form 1004 6-93

The FSBO's Closing Checklist

Figure 13.1 *(Continued)*

Lapeer Appraisal, Inc.

UNIFORM RESIDENTIAL APPRAISAL REPORT File No. 0515212

Valuation Section

ESTIMATED SITE VALUE	= $ 30,000		
ESTIMATED REPRODUCTION COST-NEW OF IMPROVEMENTS:			
Dwelling 1,409 Sq. Ft. @ $ 78.97 = $ 111,269			
Bsmt. 630 Sq. Ft. @ $ 15.10 = 9,513			
Porch/Cntrl Air = 5,000			
Garage/Carport 576 Sq. Ft. @ $ 19.87 = 11,445			
Total Estimated Cost New = $ 137,227			
Less 70 Physical	Functional	External Est. Remaining Econ. Life: 70	
Depreciation 0% = $ 0			
Depreciated Value of Improvements = $ 137,227			
"As-is" Value of Site Improvements = $ 2,500			
INDICATED VALUE BY COST APPROACH = $ 169,700			

Comments on Cost Approach (such as, source of cost estimate, site value, square foot calculation and for HUD, VA and FmHA, the estimated remaining economic life of the property): The cost approach is based on the Marshall Valuation Service and is adapted to local conditions. The contributory value of the paved drive is included in the site improvements value of the cost approach.

Sales Comparison Analysis

ITEM	SUBJECT	COMPARABLE NO. 1	+ (-) $ Adjustment	COMPARABLE NO. 2	+ (-) $ Adjustment	COMPARABLE NO. 3	+ (-) $ Adjustment
Address	827 Gardenia Davison	2106 Akram Court Davison		2229 Horseshoe Drive Davison		11118 Alexandria Lane Davison	
Proximity to Subject		1.9 MI WNW		1.5 MI W		1.1 MI SE	
Sales Price	$ 166,965	$ 181,675		$ 178,200		$ 180,500	
Price/Gross Liv. Area	$ 118.50 ⌀	$ 125.29 ⌀		$ 117.24 ⌀		$ 95.50 ⌀	
Data and/or	Interior/Exterior	MLS		MLS		MLS	
Verification Sources	Inspection	Exterior Inspection		Exterior Inspection		Exterior Inspection	
VALUE ADJUSTMENTS	DESCRIPTION	DESCRIPTION	+ (-) $ Adjustment	DESCRIPTION	+ (-) $ Adjustment	DESCRIPTION	+ (-) $ Adjustment
Sales or Financing Concessions	N/A	Conv	0	Conv	0	Conv	0
Date of Sale/Time	pending	11/10/2004	0	10/14/2004	0	02/04/2005	0
Location	City/Urban	Suburban	0	Suburban	0	Suburban	0
Leasehold/Fee Simple	Fee Simple	Fee Simple	0	Fee Simple	0	Fee Simple	0
Site	.18 Acres +/-	.23 Acre	-3,500	.23 Acre	-3,500	.15 Acre	0
View	Neighborhood	Neighborhood	0	Neighborhood	0	Neighborhood	0
Design and Appeal	2 Story/Avg	2 Story/Avg	0	2 Story/Avg	0	2 Story/Avg	0
Quality of Construction	Good	Average	0	Average	0	Average	0
Age	Yr. Blt.: 2005	2004	0	2004	0	2004	0
Condition	Good	Good	0	Good	0	Good	0
Above Grade Room Count	Total 20 Bdrms 6 Baths 3 2.50	Total 5 Bdrms 3 Baths 2.00	1,000	Total 5 Bdrms 3 Baths 2.00	1,000	Total 6 Bdrms 4 Baths 2.50	0
Gross Living Area	1,409 Sq.Ft.	1,450 Sq.Ft.	-800	1,520 Sq.Ft.	-2,200	1,890 Sq.Ft.	-9,600
Basement & Finished Rooms Below Grade	Full Basement 0% Finished	Full Basement 0% Finished	0	Full Basement 0% Finished	0	Full Basement 0% Finished	0
Functional Utility	Average	Average	0	Average	0	Average	0
Heating/Cooling	NGFA/Cntrl Air	NGFA/None	1,500	NGFA/None	1,500	NGFA/None	1,500
Energy Efficient Items	None	None	0	None	0	None	0
Garage/Carport	2 Att. Garage	2 Att. Garage	0	2 Att. Garage	0	2 Att. Garage	0
Porch, Patio, Deck, Fireplace(s), etc.	Covered Porch None	Cvrd Porch/Deck Fireplace	-1,000 -1,500	Cvrd Porch/Deck Fireplace	-1,000 -1,500	Cvrd Porch/Deck Fireplace	-1,000 -1,500
Fence, Pool, etc.	None	None	0	None	0	None	0
Amenities	Paved Drive	Paved Drive	0	Paved Drive	0	Paved Drive	0
Net Adj. (total)		☐ + ☒ - $	4,300	☐ + ☒ - $	5,700	☐ + ☒ - $	10,600
Adjusted Sales Price of Comparable		Gross: 5.1% Net: -2.4% $ 177,500		Gross: 6.0% Net: -3.2% $ 172,500		Gross: 7.5% Net: -5.9% $ 170,000	

Comments on Sales Comparison (including the subject property's compatibility to the neighborhood, etc.): All comparable sales are closed to the best of the appraiser's knowledge. Verification is with buyer, seller, realtor, agent or MLS. All images in this report are digital photos. These images are true representations and have not been changed, altered, or digitally enhanced. When transmitted by EDI format, the signatures in this report are signed by means of a digital signature file. It is noted that all three comparable sales are located more than 1 mile from the subject property, and that comparable # 2 closed more than six months prior to the date of appraisal. The sales chosen are the most similar available. See Addendum

ITEM	SUBJECT	COMPARABLE NO. 1	COMPARABLE NO. 2	COMPARABLE NO. 3
Date, Price and Data Source for prior sales within year of appraisal	see below*	see below*	see below*	see below*

Analysis of any current agreement of sale, option, or listing of the subject property and analysis of any prior sales of subject and comparables within one year of the date of appraisal: See Attached Addendum

Reconciliation

INDICATED VALUE BY SALES COMPARISON APPROACH .... $ 172,500

INDICATED VALUE BY INCOME APPROACH (If Applicable) Estimated Market Rent $ _____ /Mo. x Gross Rent Multiplier _____ = $ N/A

This appraisal is made ☐ "as is" ☐ subject to the repairs, alterations, inspections or conditions listed below ☒ subject to completion per plans and specifications.

Conditions of Appraisal: This appraisal is based on the satisfactory completion of the dwelling according to the plans included in this report. See Addendum

Final Reconciliation: The market approach and the cost approach were correlated to arrive at the estimated value. More weight was given to the sales approach as I feel that it is a more accurate indication of the actual market's perception of the value of a property. The income approach was not utilized due to the lack of rental data in the area for this type of property.

The purpose of this appraisal is to estimate the market value of the real property that is the subject of this report, based on the above conditions and the certification, contingent and limiting conditions, and market value definition that are stated in the attached Freddie Mac Form 439/Fannie Mae Form 1004B (Revised 6/93).

I (WE) ESTIMATE THE MARKET VALUE, AS DEFINED, OF THE REAL PROPERTY THAT IS THE SUBJECT OF THIS REPORT, AS OF 04/14/2005 (WHICH IS THE DATE OF INSPECTION AND THE EFFECTIVE DATE OF THIS REPORT) TO BE $ 172,500 .

APPRAISER:	SUPERVISORY APPRAISER (ONLY IF REQUIRED):	
Signature	Signature	☐ Did ☐ Did Not
Name Dale R. Hager	Name	Inspect Property
Date Report Signed 04/21/2005	Date Report Signed	
State Certification # 1201000677 State MI	State Certification #	State
Or State License # State	Or State License #	State

Freddie Mac Form 70 6-93

PAGE 2 OF 2
Produced using ACI software, 800.234.8727 www.aciweb.com

Fannie Mae Form 1004 6-93

Lapeer Appraisal Inc.

Appraisal Requirements

In virtually all residential real estate transactions, an appraisal is required. This is especially true if a third party lender is providing the financing. A professional opinion of value issued by a licensed appraiser serves as the basis by which lenders make financing decisions. Before a lender can loan money for the purchase of a house, he or she must know what the value of that house is. For obvious reasons, lenders cannot rely on what a buyer or seller may think their house is worth. They must instead rely on the professional estimate of value issued by an unbiased third party who is licensed to render such an opinion. A certified appraisal gives the lender the confidence needed to provide financing for housing in areas that he or she may have no firsthand knowledge of. The level of confidence an appraisal offers is so high that the lender can, in fact, provide financing on a national scale.

If no third party financing is needed, then an appraisal may not be required. For example, if you sell your house on what is known as a *land contract*, then the decision to hire an appraiser is up to you and the buyer. If you're not already familiar with the term *land contract*, it is the same thing as owner financing. For example, if you own your house free and clear and want to finance the sale of it to the buyer by allowing her to make payments directly to you, then you are selling your house on a land contract. In some instances, even if you don't own your house free and clear, you may still be able to sell it using a land contract by creating what is referred to as a *wrap-around mortgage*. When a wrap-around mortgage is used, the underlying mortgage is not paid off at the time of closing. Instead, the buyer makes payments directly to the seller, while the seller continues to make payments to the original lender. The seller is then entitled to keep the difference between the two payments, if, in fact, there is any. Just last week I represented a client of mine who sold his house using that very technique. In this particular example, he owed as much as his house was worth, so the difference between what the buyer will pay him and what he is now paying to the lender is minimal. Because the buyer and the seller were both in agreement as to the value of the house, and the seller is providing the financing directly to the buyer, they both agreed that no appraisal was necessary. You should keep in mind, however, that my client's situation is the exception rather than the rule. In most instances, your house will need to be appraised by a licensed professional.

Appraisals, CMAs, and BPOs

Recall from Chapter 4 that a comparative market analysis, or CMA, is frequently used by real estate agents to form an estimate of value. Although CMAs can provide a good estimate of value, they are a dime a dozen, and most agents will gladly do them free of charge for prospective clients, in hopes of getting the clients to sign a listing agreement. An appraiser, on the other hand, follows an established set of rules and guidelines that provide for a more objective and exact estimate of value. While a CMA and an appraisal both provide estimates of value, an appraisal is generally said to be more exact because it is done by a professional who has been specially trained to evaluate real property. Lenders typically will not accept a CMA. Instead, lenders almost always require an appraisal. There are some instances when lenders will accept what is known as a *broker's price opinion*, or BPO. A BPO, which is much the same as a comparative market analysis that real estate agents provide to their clients, is used by lenders to obtain a rough estimate of value in certain circumstances. For example, if a lender has foreclosed on a house and it is now listed as a nonperforming asset on the bank's books, the lender may request a BPO to get an idea of what the property would sell for. Because a BPO provides only a rough estimate of value and is not nearly as precise as an actual appraisal, the advantages to a lender of using a BPO rather than an appraisal under these circumstances are twofold. First, a BPO doesn't take as long to complete as an appraisal, and second, a BPO doesn't cost as much as an appraisal. In all likelihood, when it comes time to sell your house, neither a BPO or a CMA will be acceptable to a lending institution. You should instead plan on having an appraisal done.

How to Get the Buyer to Pay for the Appraisal

Virtually all expenses related to a real estate transaction are negotiable, including the appraisal. A case can easily be made to the buyer, however, that he should be responsible for paying for the appraisal because it is his lender who will require it. Buyers will most likely obtain new loans to purchase a house and, when they do, the lenders they use will require that appraisals be done. As previously explained, the lender requires that an estimate of value be provided by a licensed appraiser to help determine how much can be loaned. Having the buyer pay for the appraisal can best be addressed by putting the language into the purchase agreement ahead of time. For example, a clause should be included in the section provided for financing that says the buyer is responsible for any and all costs related to obtaining the loan. This would include the cost of an appraisal, since it is the lender who requires it. If the language is already embodied within the contract, chances are buyers will not challenge it, and even if they do, simply remind them that it is their lender that is requiring the appraisal.

Scheduling and Preparing for the Appraisal

Depending on the area in which you live, the appraisal may need to be scheduled several weeks in advance. If the real estate market in your area is fairly strong, then in all likelihood most of the services related to it will require additional time for scheduling. On the other hand, if the market in your area is only moderately strong, then it may be possible to get an appraisal in as little as a week. In most instances, because it is the lender who will order the appraisal, you won't have to be overly concerned about this. It is a good idea, however, to be aware of this requirement for two reasons. The first reason is that as the homeowner you will need to be available to let the appraiser into your house. Although much of the evaluation work is done outside of your home, the appraiser will still need access to the inside of it to determine its overall condition, measure the rooms to obtain accurate square footage data, and note any special features such as options and upgrades that may add value to it. This process typically does not require more than an hour. The second reason is that, as the seller, you want to be aware of the progress the buyer is making toward purchasing your house. A key element of obtaining a new loan is having an appraisal done. If you haven't heard from the buyer or the lender about scheduling an appraisal, then it's a good idea to follow up just to be sure that everyone is working together and that this essential step has not been overlooked.

The FSBO's Closing Checklist

When preparing for the appraisal, you should be aware of these two important steps. First, as the seller, you want your house to show well to help the appraiser form as favorable an opinion as possible. The better your house shows, the more value the appraiser can give you, especially when it is compared to other houses that may not show as well. Getting your house ready to show at this juncture in the sales process should not be difficult at all, because by now, you have already made all the necessary preparations to make it presentable to buyers. The second important step to be aware of is that the appraiser will measure almost all of the interior rooms in your house. If there is a lot of clutter throughout the house or anything else that might be in the appraiser's way, be courteous enough to remove such things so that the measurements of each room can be easily taken. Remember that the appraiser is forming an opinion of your house as it relates to value, so it is in your best interest to make his job as easy as you can.

In summary, an appraisal is an essential part of almost every real estate transaction, especially if a lender is providing the financing. The most common method of appraisal used for estimating the value of residential property is the sales comparison method, which is based on the premise of substitution. Although CMAs and BPOs serve useful functions, a professional opinion from a certified appraiser is required by most lenders. Finally, you'll want to coordinate your schedule with that of the appraiser to make your house available for inspection.

14

Closing the Sale: How to Make Sure Your Closing Goes as Smoothly as Possible

The closing is the point in time when all of the parties that have an interest in the sale of your house come together to finalize the transaction. You have likely spent a good deal of time and money preparing your house to sell: you have advertised and marketed it in the appropriate places and you have found a buyer who is ready, willing, and able to purchase it. It is now time to get ready for the closing. In an effort to ensure as smooth and trouble-free a closing as possible, there are several steps that should be taken prior to the actual date of the closing. These include scheduling a closing date with the appropriate parties, providing the title company with updated information, and coordinating various tasks with the buyer. In addition to these duties, you can further prepare yourself for the closing by becoming familiar with settlement statements and the various charges that buyers and sellers are customarily responsible for.

Scheduling the Appropriate Parties

In the purchase agreement, or sales contract, there is a provision for the closing date that states the purchase of the house is "to close by" a particular date that you and the buyer agree on at that time. The date listed in the agreement, however, will not necessarily be the same date as the actual closing. Although the two dates can be the same, the date given in the contract is more of a general guideline, or a target date, by which both parties agree to close. Although the sale can close any time prior to the date listed in the agreement, both parties have agreed and are contractually obligated to ensure that the closing does not occur after the date in the contract. It is therefore important to begin coordinating with the title company, the buyer, the buyer's mortgage company, your mortgage company, and your attorney (if one is used) as early as possible. Depending on the area in which you live and the various parties involved, 30 days is usually sufficient notice. There are some instances, however, when as long as 45 or even 60 days may be required. For example, if there are unresolved issues affecting the title of your house, or if the buyer is having to work through some credit problems, then more time may be required.

Scheduling a closing date begins with the title company. You must first verify with their scheduler what times and dates they have available. Depending on the title company you are using, there may be a great deal of flexibility with scheduling, or it may be booked solid for the next two or three weeks. The limited availability of closing appointments can be frustrating for clients because they are trying to bring several people together at one time, which can sometimes be difficult to do. Although I've had to stand in line to schedule a closing in the past, I bring enough business to title companies that this is no longer the case. In fact, the title companies now stand in line in an effort to earn my company's business.

Once a closing date has been confirmed with the title company, the next step is to coordinate that date with the buyer. The buyer will in turn need to notify his or her mortgage company of the date so that the lender can ensure that all of the necessary documentation will be completed in time. If a loan has been approved "with conditions," as most loans are, the buyer will need to be sure all of those conditions have been satisfied. Sometimes satisfying the loan conditions is a fairly simple process and requires nothing more than providing buyers with proof of insurance, for example. Other times, however, satisfying loan conditions may be quite involved and may, for example, require the buyer to verify certain information listed on the application such as the source of a down payment. In any event, the sooner you can agree on a date for the closing with the buyer, the more smoothly your transaction is likely to go.

After you've coordinated the closing date with the buyer, if you are having an attorney represent you at the closing, he or she will also need to be notified of the date. If you're not having an attorney represent you at the closing, but are having an attorney review all of the legal documents, then this is not as big an issue. You will still need to coordinate the timing with him or her, however, so that all of the necessary documents the attorney's office is responsible for will be ready in time. Finally, you'll need to notify your mortgage company of the impending sale so that they, too, can begin preparing the file. The main thing the title company will need from your lender is the *loan payoff*. The information in a loan payoff is used to disburse funds at the closing to the lender to ensure that the loan is paid in full and that all outstanding obligations have been satisfied. The loan payoff is issued by the mortgage company and states pertinent information related to the loan including the following items:

- Loan number
- Property address
- Mortgagor's name (borrower)
- Mortgagee's name (lender)
- Prepayment penalties, if any
- Remaining loan balance
- Accrued interest
- Late charges
- Recording fees
- Processing fees
- Overnight fees

Depending on the title company you are working with and the level of service it provides, it may or may not contact the lender directly to request a loan payoff. If the title company does request the information from the lender, you will still need to be prepared to give the closing agent relevant information about the loan so that it can then request it from the lender. Regardless of who requests the loan payoff, it is essential for you to be aware of this important step so that the loan obligation can be appropriately satisfied at the time of closing. If you've taken out a second mortgage against your house, as many homeowners have, then the title company will also need a loan payoff from that mortgagor as well. I recommend asking the title company for a copy of the loan payoff well in advance of the date of closing so that you have the opportunity to review it for accuracy.

Current Tax Information

In addition to having a loan payoff, your title company will need a sort of tax payoff. The title company will verify with the appropriate government tax authorities what amount of taxes are owed on your property, if any, at the time of closing. In some states, taxes are paid in arrears, meaning that they are paid for a previous period. For example, an individual may receive a tax bill on January 1 for taxes owed that will in turn be applied toward the previous year. In other states, taxes are prepaid, meaning they are paid for the upcoming period. Using the same example, the tax bill received on January 1 would be for the coming year instead of the previous one. If the taxes are paid in arrears in your state, then there's a good chance the buyer will receive a credit from you for the portion of time you owned the property. On the other hand, if you live in a state in which the taxes are prepaid, then as long as your taxes are current, you will receive a credit from the buyer at the time of closing for the period of time the buyer will own the house through the end of the period in which the taxes have been paid. Regardless of whether or not taxes are paid in advance or arrears, the title company is responsible for obtaining the information from the appropriate taxing authorities. Generally speaking, you do not need to be concerned with this aspect of the closing because the title company will handle it for you. There are occasions, however, when a discrepancy exists regarding the amount owed according to the taxing authority, so it is a good idea to review this information prior to the closing. The closing agent responsible for your file can easily provide the tax information to you. All you have to do is ask for it.

Clear to Close

One term or phrase you should be familiar with is a *clear to close*. A clear to close is the term used by the buyer's lender signifying that all conditions pertaining to the loan have been satisfied. In virtually all loans that are made, there are specific conditions that must be met prior to the closing. Examples of these conditions include verification of the following items:

- Credit history: review of history and verification of credit scores
- Employment: verification of place of employment, length of time, and position or title
- Income: verification of salary, wages, and any other bonuses
- Tax returns: previous two or three years may be required
- Checking accounts: generally three monthly statements covering the last 90 days
- Savings accounts: generally three monthly statements covering the last 90 days
- Retirement accounts: generally three monthly statements covering the last 90 days
- Homeowner's insurance policy with adequate coverage
- Delinquent taxes that may be owed
- Past due accounts that must be brought current

Once all of the lender's conditions have been satisfied, a clear to close can then be issued. The clear to close essentially gives the title company a green light to proceed with the closing. When the closer notifies you that a clear to close has been issued, you know you're in the home stretch and that the closing is only a few days away!

Utility and Services Transfers

As soon as a firm closing date has been established, you'll want to notify all of the utility companies that are providing you with service of the impending sale so that service can be transferred at the appropriate time. The following is a checklist of companies that should be notified if their services are being used.

- Electric company
- Natural gas company

- Liquefied gas companies providing propane, butane, or heating oil
- Water and sewer department of the local municipality providing these services
- Sanitation services for waste and garbage pickup
- Cable and satellite providers
- Telephone company
- High speed cable or DSL service
- Delivery services such as bottled water
- Post office
- Insurance company providing homeowner's policy
- Any other companies that may be providing you with service specific to your residence

The effective date of the transfer is typically the date of possession. This may or may not be the same day as the day of closing. If the buyer is planning to move in on the day of the closing and you have already moved out, then the date of possession is the same day as the date of closing. In this instance, the effective date for the transfer of utilities is the same day as the day you close. If, on the other hand, you have agreed with the buyer to remain in the house for several days after the date of closing so that you can finish moving, then the effective date for transferring the utilities should be the date on which you will be out of the house. From that time forward, the new owner will be responsible for them if applicable. In most instances, utility services such as natural gas and electric are usually left on with only a transfer of name occurring. If the property is going to sit vacant for a while, however, the utility company may actually disconnect or terminate the service. Some utility companies require that both parties call in to verify that services will be transferred to a new owner, while other companies only require either the buyer or the seller to notify them. In any event, be sure to plan ahead by contacting each company at least several days in advance so that they will have adequate time to make the requested changes.

Understanding the Settlement Statement

The Department of Housing and Urban Development, or HUD, uses a standardized form to show all of the funds disbursed at closing. This form, commonly referred to as a HUD statement, settlement statement, or closing statement, is typically prepared by the title company handling the closing. The form details line by line all of the associated debits and credits assessed to both buyer and seller. These charges, or disbursements, are itemized in two columns—one for the seller and one for the buyer. The following checklist provides a sample of a few of the more common items found on a settlement statement, but it is by no means an exhaustive list.

- Contract sales price
- Earnest money deposit
- Principal amount of new loan(s)
- Payoff of existing loan(s)
- Seller financing
- Prorated tax adjustments
- Prorated home owner association dues
- Prorated rental or income adjustments if applicable
- Lender fees including credit report, underwriting, loan origination, and application charges
- Title insurance charges
- Home inspection costs
- Home warranty charges
- Termite inspection fees
- Appraisal charges
- Survey charges
- Legal fees
- Recording fees
- Overnight mailing or shipping charges
- Bank wire fees for direct deposit of seller proceeds

You should be provided with a preliminary copy of the HUD statement by the title company at least 24 hours prior to the closing. The HUD statement will have listed on it all of the disbursements, or payments, made to the various parties who have an interest in the sale of your house. It is important for you to review each charge listed on the seller's side of the closing statement that pertains to you to verify its accuracy. You don't have to be overly concerned with the buyer's side of the closing statement because those items don't necessarily affect you.

The FSBO's Closing Checklist

Reviewing your side of the closing statement for accuracy is your chief concern. Let the buyer take care of his or her side. In many situations, separate HUD statements are prepared for the seller and the buyer. The seller's statement lists only those items pertaining to you, while the buyer's statement lists only those items pertaining to him or her. Providing separate closing statements helps maintain each party's confidentiality, so, for example, the buyer wouldn't know how much cash the seller is walking away with after the closing and the seller wouldn't know how much the buyer is borrowing.

The reason it's important for you to review the closing statement prior to the closing is because you want to verify its accuracy *before* the actual closing. By allowing time prior to the closing to correct any errors that may have been made, the closing itself will go much smoother. This is much better than sitting down at the closing table with the buyer and discovering that an error was made and then having the closing agent try to work through it at that time. Errors are inadvertently made for one reason or another. For example, the title company may have the incorrect payoff amount for your loan, or the taxes may not be prorated correctly, or there may have been a credit to either you or the buyer that was not properly applied. Don't assume for even a single moment that because the closing officer is experienced and acts as the facilitator in numerous closings that "she must be right because she is the closer and she should know." Precisely the opposite is true. Because the closer does act as the facilitator in numerous closings, it is all the more reason she must rely on you to provide accurate information for the settlement statement. The potential risk to you of failing to review the settlement statement can be substantial and potentially cost you hundreds or even thousands of dollars. On virtually every property I've bought or sold, there has been an error of one type or another on the settlement statement. Although sometimes the errors are very minor and take only a few minutes to correct, other times they are quite significant and can take several hours, or even days, to resolve. By correcting discrepancies prior to the closing, much of the stress that sometimes occurs during this time can be alleviated. If all of the documents, including the settlement statement, are correct, then the closing process will go smoothly and any additional stress will be avoided. When everything is in order, the process becomes more of a formality as the closing officer obtains all of the necessary signatures on the proper forms to transfer the property from one party to the other. (See Figure 14.1.)

Review and Verify the Accuracy of Prorated Items

Recall from Chapter 10 the discussion of *prorating* as used in the sales agreement. That section is especially important in this chapter because the HUD statement is where prorations are applied. Remember that to prorate is to apportion costs or expenses associated with the property that become effective the date of the transfer, which is usually the same day as the day of closing. Common expenses that are prorated include taxes, association fees, maintenance fees, rental income, and any other income or expense specifically related to the property. When an item is prorated, it is apportioned or assigned to the party responsible for it based upon the date of ownership. Let's review the example used in Chapter 10. If a seller prepaid $3,000 in taxes for the current year beginning January 1, and the closing occurred on June 30, then the seller would be entitled to receive a credit at closing as follows:

$$(\$3,000/365) \times (365 - 181) =$$
$$\$8.21917 \times 184 = \$1,512.33$$

The seller in this example would be entitled to receive a credit on the day of closing for the remaining balance of the tax that has already been paid at a rate of roughly $8.22 per diem, or per day, because she has prepaid the taxes in advance for the current year. The per diem rate is then multiplied by the number of days prepaid to calculate the credit due her. In this example, the seller would be entitled to receive a credit of $1,512.33. This figure is then listed on the closing statement as a credit to the seller and a debit to the buyer. The buyer is essentially reimbursing the seller for taxes that have already been paid. In your review of the settlement statement for accuracy prior to closing, be sure to review all of the prorated items on the statement and verify them for accuracy as well.

The FSBO's Closing Checklist

Figure 14.1   Settlement Statement

A. **Settlement Statement**	U.S. Department of Housing and Urban Development	OMB Approval No. 2502-0265

B. Type of Loan

1. ☐ FHA 2. ☐ FmHA 3. ☐ Conv. Unins. 4. ☐ VA 5. ☐ Conv. Ins.	6. File Number:	7. Loan Number:	8. Mortgage Insurance Case Number:

C. Note: This form is furnished to give you a statement of actual settlement costs. Amounts paid to and by the settlement agent are shown. Items marked "(p.o.c.)" were paid outside the closing; they are shown here for informational purposes and are not included in the totals.

D. Name & Address of Borrower:	E. Name & Address of Seller:	F. Name & Address of Lender:

G. Property Location:	H. Settlement Agent:	
	Place of Settlement:	I. Settlement Date:

J. Summary of Borrower's Transaction		K. Summary of Seller's Transaction	
100. Gross Amount Due From Borrower		**400. Gross Amount Due To Seller**	
101. Contract sales price		401. Contract sales price	
102. Personal property		402. Personal property	
103. Settlement charges to borrower (line 1400)		403.	
104.		404.	
105.		405.	
Adjustments for items paid by seller in advance		**Adjustments for items paid by seller in advance**	
106. City/town taxes to		406. City/town taxes to	
107. County taxes to		407. County taxes to	
108. Assessments to		408. Assessments to	
109.		409.	
110.		410.	
111.		411.	
112.		412.	
120. Gross Amount Due From Borrower		**420. Gross Amount Due To Seller**	
200. Amounts Paid By Or In Behalf Of Borrower		**500. Reductions In Amount Due To Seller**	
201. Deposit or earnest money		501. Excess deposit (see instructions)	
202. Principal amount of new loan(s)		502. Settlement charges to seller (line 1400)	
203. Existing loan(s) taken subject to		503. Existing loan(s) taken subject to	
204.		504. Payoff of first mortgage loan	
205.		505. Payoff of second mortgage loan	
206.		506.	
207.		507.	
208.		508.	
209.		509.	
Adjustments for items unpaid by seller		**Adjustments for items unpaid by seller**	
210. City/town taxes to		510. City/town taxes to	
211. County taxes to		511. County taxes to	
212. Assessments to		512. Assessments to	
213.		513.	
214.		514.	
215.		515.	
216.		516.	
217.		517.	
218.		518.	
219.		519.	
220. Total Paid By/For Borrower		**520. Total Reduction Amount Due Seller**	
300. Cash At Settlement From/To Borrower		**600. Cash At Settlement To/From Seller**	
301. Gross Amount due from borrower (line 120)		601. Gross amount due to seller (line 420)	
302. Less amounts paid by/for borrower (line 220)	( )	602. Less reductions in amt. due seller (line 520)	( )
303. Cash ☐ From ☐ To Borrower		**603. Cash** ☐ To ☐ From Seller	

Section 5 of the Real Estate Settlement Procedures Act (RESPA) requires the following: • HUD must develop a Special Information Booklet to help persons borrowing money to finance the purchase of residential real estate to better understand the nature and costs of real estate settlement services; • Each lender must provide the booklet to all applicants from whom it receives or for whom it prepares a written application to borrow money to finance the purchase of residential real estate; • Lenders must prepare and distribute with the Booklet a Good Faith Estimate of the settlement costs that the borrower is likely to incur in connection with the settlement. These disclosures are manadatory.

Section 4(a) of RESPA mandates that HUD develop and prescribe this standard form to be used at the time of loan settlement to provide full disclosure of all charges imposed upon the borrower and seller. These are third party disclosures that are designed to provide the borrower with pertinent information during the settlement process in order to be a better shopper.

The Public Reporting Burden for this collection of information is estimated to average one hour per response, including the time for reviewing instructions, searching existing data sources, gathering and maintaining the data needed, and completing and reviewing the collection of information.

This agency may not collect this information, and you are not required to complete this form, unless it displays a currently valid OMB control number.

The information requested does not lend itself to confidentiality.

Closing the Sale

Figure 14.1 *(Continued)*

L. Settlement Charges

			Paid From Borrowers Funds at Settlement	Paid From Seller's Funds at Settlement
700. Total Sales/Broker's Commission based on price $	@	% =		
Division of Commission (line 700) as follows:				
701. $	to			
702. $	to			
703. Commission paid at Settlement				
704.				
800. Items Payable In Connection With Loan				
801. Loan Origination Fee	%			
802. Loan Discount	%			
803. Appraisal Fee	to			
804. Credit Report	to			
805. Lender's Inspection Fee				
806. Mortgage Insurance Application Fee to				
807. Assumption Fee				
808.				
809.				
810.				
811.				
900. Items Required By Lender To Be Paid In Advance				
901. Interest from	to	@$	/day	
902. Mortgage Insurance Premium for		months to		
903. Hazard Insurance Premium for		years to		
904.		years to		
905.				
1000. Reserves Deposited With Lender				
1001. Hazard insurance	months @ $	per month		
1002. Mortgage insurance	months @ $	per month		
1003. City property taxes	months @ $	per month		
1004. County property taxes	months @ $	per month		
1005. Annual assessments	months @ $	per month		
1006.	months @ $	per month		
1007.	months @ $	per month		
1008.	months @ $	per month		
1100. Title Charges				
1101. Settlement or closing fee	to			
1102. Abstract or title search	to			
1103. Title examination	to			
1104. Title insurance binder	to			
1105. Document preparation	to			
1106. Notary fees	to			
1107. Attorney's fees	to			
(includes above items numbers:		)		
1108. Title insurance	to			
(includes above items numbers:		)		
1109. Lender's coverage	$			
1110. Owner's coverage	$			
1111.				
1112.				
1113.				
1200. Government Recording and Transfer Charges				
1201. Recording fees: Deed $	; Mortgage $	; Releases $		
1202. City/county tax/stamps: Deed $	; Mortgage $			
1203. State tax/stamps: Deed $	; Mortgage $			
1204.				
1205.				
1300. Additional Settlement Charges				
1301. Survey	to			
1302. Pest inspection to				
1303.				
1304.				
1305.				
1400. Total Settlement Charges (enter on lines 103, Section J and 502, Section K)				

Final Walk-Through Inspection

One stipulation often found in sales contracts is the right of the buyer to perform a final walk-through inspection of your house just prior to the close. The walk-through inspection should be scheduled no sooner than one day before the closing date and can be scheduled as late as the morning of the closing. The final inspection is not intended to give the buyers an excuse or reason not to follow through with the purchase of your house. It is instead designed to protect them by giving them the right to one last inspection before the closing to verify that the property is in as good as or better condition than when it was placed under contract. Without this right, it would be very easy for something to break down and not get repaired by the seller. For example, suppose the furnace went out a week before the closing. An unscrupulous seller may try to get by without repairing it, knowing that in just a few more days it would no longer be his problem. Allowing the buyer one last opportunity to inspect a house helps prevent exactly this type of situation. The final walk-through should not be nearly as exhaustive or thorough as when the house was inspected by a certified professional. Rather, a brief tour of the house and test of major appliances and plumbing is all that is required. Be sure to plan ahead by coordinating with the buyer when the final inspection is to take place so that the necessary time can be set aside in advance for this important step.

Closing Day

The big day has finally come! It's now time to meet with the closing agent, the buyers, and the attorney (if one is being used) to finalize the sale of your house! While the actual closing process generally takes less than an hour, it can take as long as two or three hours. The closing agent usually meets with the buyer and seller separately at first because of the confidentiality of the various documents being signed. For example, there may be sensitive material contained in the buyers' loan documents that they prefer to keep private. The closing agent typically meets with the buyers first to obtain all of the necessary signatures. Once the buyers have signed off on everything, the closing agent will then meet with you to review the sale and to obtain your signature as needed. After everything has been signed, the closing agent will then need to contact the buyers' lender to obtain a funding number before disbursing funds. Copies of all the documents you have signed are generally made during that time as well. While this is being done, the closing agent will often bring the buyer and the seller together to exchange any last minute information or items. This is also a good time to provide the buyers with a set of keys to their new home. As soon as a funding number has been obtained from the lender, the closing agent can present your check to you for whatever funds are owed. At this point, you're all done with the closing. Congratulations! You've just sold your house without a real estate agent.

15

Moving Preparations: How to Plan Your Move without Getting Ahead of Yourself

Now that your home is sold, the real fun is about to begin! That's right, it's time to move. If you wait until the date of closing to plan and prepare for your move, however, you have waited too long. Planning a move requires careful preparation well in advance of the closing date. The move out date and subsequent date of possession by the purchaser must be coordinated with the buyer and either a professional moving company, a container service, or a truck rental service. Although it is wise to plan your moving date in advance, you should be aware of certain pitfalls of doing so prematurely. Finally, termination of various services must also be planned carefully prior to the date of moving.

Careful Planning Must Be Balanced with Awareness

The date of possession, which is stipulated in the purchase agreement, is the date that you officially turn over your house to the new owners. Although the date of possession is sometimes the same day as the closing, you may find that you need an additional two or three days to finish packing and get all of your belongings moved. You should coordinate the moving date with the new buyer, who will also be scheduling and planning in the move. Even though the date of possession was originally established in the purchase agreement, you and the buyer may need to be somewhat flexible and continue to work together so that both sets of needs are met. For example, the rental truck or moving company that you had lined up in advance may push your date back by a day or two because of a weather delay, broken down equipment, or any number of other reasons. The point is that you must be prepared to work together to allow time for you to get out of the house and to allow the buyer time to get in.

One pitfall you should be aware of when planning a move is not to get ahead of yourself in the process. I know, I know. I just finished saying in the previous paragraph that you should plan your move well in advance. That statement must be balanced, however, with the cautionary note that you shouldn't get ahead of yourself. The danger of getting everything packed too far in advance is that anything can happen in the interim, meaning that the sale of your house might fall through for any number of reasons. For example, while the buyer's ability to obtain financing may have looked promising in the beginning, it may turn out that he or she doesn't qualify for a loan after all. Or, if the buyer found another house that she liked better, she may begin to look for excuses to delay the closing, and eventually not close at all. While it is true that she may be in default of the agreement, this is a very real possibility. Sometimes you can detect these unexpected events by communicating with both the title company and the buyer, and other times you cannot. The key is to be constantly be aware of events as they transpire throughout the closing process. If you already have all of your belongings packed up and, worse yet, have already started moving some items to your new house, your efforts could quite possibly be frustrated by a buyer who, for one reason or another, may not be able to purchase your house.

Sometimes, no matter how well you plan, things just don't work out the way they're supposed to. Let's look at an example of what can go wrong, even after careful planning. I have two buyers I am working with who were supposed to close in back-to-back closings this morning. The first buyer, Mr. R, is buying a new home from Symphony Homes and the second buyer, Mrs. T, is buying Mr. R's house. Mr. R needs the proceeds from the sale of his house before he can purchase one of our new homes because the equity for his new home is coming from the sale of his current one. Unfortunately, Mrs. T has not received a clear to close yet from the mortgage company she is working with. Even though we've had both of these closings scheduled for three weeks, the lender failed to prepare the documents in time because the loan is still in underwriting. Until all of the underwriting department's conditions have been satisfied, the loan cannot close. Meanwhile, Mr. R already has a moving service lined up for this weekend, and the utilities are scheduled to be shut off at his existing house in two days. To top it off, he had a week of vacation scheduled so that he would have plenty of time to get settled into his new home. Needless to say, Mr. R is not at all happy about the delay. In fact, it's safe to say that he is quite livid. In this example, it's safe to assume that both of these transactions will take place because Mrs. T is a solid buyer with a credit score of 800+ and plenty of cash to put down. Through no fault of the seller, however, both sales have been delayed, and both parties must continue to remain flexible.

My intention in this section is not to dampen your enthusiasm when you are so close to getting your house sold, but rather to bring to your attention the possibility that sometimes things don't work out the way we hope they will. It is wise to plan ahead and be ready for the big moving day, but balance that planning by keeping the lines of communication open with the buyer and the title company and by being aware of the closing process as it transpires.

Timing Your Move

Whether you're using a professional moving company, a container service, or a truck rental service, it is best to schedule a date with the company as far in advance as possible. As a general rule, moving companies and truck rental companies tend to be the busiest toward the end of the month and on weekends because that is when the majority of moves occur. People tend to move at the end of the month because that is when the next rent payment or house payment is due. Weekends are also popular times to move because many people don't have to work then, which gives them additional time to move. Moving companies and rental companies are frequently booked up several weeks in advance, especially around these peak times, so don't wait until the last minute to get on the schedule.

Professional Moving Services

If you're relocating out of state or more than several hundred miles from your current location, you'll probably need to hire a professional moving company to help you. If your move is job related, such as a promotion and a transfer, there's a good chance your employer will offer a relocation package, which includes reimbursement for moving expenses. Your supervisor or human resources department can verify what benefits are available. One advantage of using a professional full-service moving company is that the company has trained individuals who will move everything for you. Services range from complete packing to moving only the large items, such as furniture and appliances. Also, because most moving companies use a large semitruck, they can move everything in one trip. This saves you from having to drive back and forth and make countless trips yourself. The primary disadvantage of using a full-service moving company is the cost. Depending on the size of your house, how full the rooms are, and how far the movers have to travel, a full-service move can easily exceed $5000.

Container Services

If you're relocating out of state and don't want to drive a rental truck yourself, an alternative to using a full-service company is to use a container service. Many trucking companies use large steel containers that can transport just about anything, including household belongings. While the majority of goods that are transported by trucking companies are for commercial enterprises, as a source of generating additional revenue, some of these companies actually cater to people who need to move. Whether they are hauling canned goods for a grocer, electronic equipment for a technology firm, or household furniture for someone who is moving makes no difference to the trucking company. They get paid regardless of what is being transported.

When my family and I moved up to Michigan from Texas, we used a container service that ended up costing less than half of the estimate we were given by full-service movers. The container service dropped off two large steel containers in front of our house about a week ahead of our scheduled move. With the help of family and friends, I was then able to load them at my convenience over the next several days. The containers, which are made of a heavy gauge steel, could be locked up at night to keep our belongings safe. After I finished loading them, the trucking service picked both containers up and pulled them both at the same time with one hooked to the other. My family and I then took our time driving to Michigan while the trucking service transported our belongings. We scheduled the containers to be dropped off at our new house a couple of days after our arrival and were then able to take our time unloading them. Using a container service like this transferred the burden of packing and loading to me and my family, but saved us several thousand dollars by doing so.

Truck Rental Services

A truck rental service is another good alternative for moving, especially if your move is local. The primary advantage to renting a truck for local moves is that it is far less expensive than using a full-service moving company. For example, a truck can usually be rented for less than $100 a day, compared to as much as several thousand dollars for a full-service company. The primary disadvantage is, of course, that you must be prepared to do all the work by yourself, with the exception of any family members and friends that you might be able to enlist for a few hours. If you are physically able, then look at this as an opportunity to get some exercise! The cargo area of rental trucks ranges in size from about 15 feet in length and 8 feet in height, to as much as 30 feet in length. The difference in cost from one size to the next is usually not that significant, so if you're like most people and have a lot of stuff to move, it's better to rent the larger size in order to minimize the number of trips you have to make.

If you're not sure exactly what size truck you'll need, the moving company can provide you with some general guidelines. When it comes to moving, I subscribe to the notion that "more is better," even if it means spending a few extra dollars. Just last week, a friend of mine named Ed moved from a house into a two bedroom apartment. He thought he could get by with a 15-foot truck, but another friend of mine and I didn't think so and recommended that he get a larger truck. Ed took our advice and rented a 27-foot truck. As it turned out, it's a good thing he did, because by the time he got the larger items such as the furniture loaded, he needed every last inch of space in the larger truck!

Termination and Transfer of Services

As you may recall, in Chapter 14 we discussed the need to plan ahead by scheduling in advance the termination of various services at the house you are moving from. The most important of these services are the utilities (refer to Chapter 14 for the complete list). These include natural gas, electricity, water and sewer, and your telephone provider. If you are relocating within the same general vicinity, then more than likely the same utility company that provided service at your old residence will also provide service to you at your new residence. Transferring utility services is very easy to do and can usually be done over the phone. Simply call the utility provider and give them the date service is to be terminated at the old residence and the date service is to be started at the new residence. Utility companies often charge a disconnect or transfer of service fee, so be sure to ask them about these and any other fees you can expect, while you're on the phone with them. If you're relocating to another area that falls outside of your current providers' area, then the new utility company may require you to complete and sign an application before the service can be turned on. Some companies also require that a deposit be made, until you have established a payment history with them. While transferring services is a relatively easy task, the most important thing to remember is to plan ahead.

Conclusion

In 2004, an all-time record number of existing houses were sold. According to the National Association of Realtors, existing home sales increased approximately 6.5 percent, bringing the total to 220,000 houses shy of 7 million. Of these, over 1 million homes were sold as FSBOs, with estimates indicating that an additional 750,000 homeowners attempted to sell their homes without using a real estate agent, bringing the total number to about 1.75 million households. The difference between success and failure for these

The FSBO's Closing Checklist

FSBOs was information, knowledge, and an understanding of what it takes to get a house sold in today's competitive market environment. There's a lot more to selling a house than simply sticking a sign in the front yard. Homeowners who want to sell their own houses must be familiar with a variety of key variables that affect the marketability of a house, including being familiar with local market conditions, knowing which home improvements will add the most value, and understanding how to price a house using a comparative market analysis. The FSBO must also be familiar with the various legal forms and documents that are needed, essential marketing strategies, and discount services provided by fee-for-sale agents. Understanding how to show a house, negotiate with buyers, and formalize the sale using the proper contracts are also essential to the FSBO. Finally, sellers must be familiar with the title insurance process, how to comply with home inspection and appraisal requirements, and, last but not least, how to prepare for and ensure a trouble-free closing. By following the steps outlined in this book, *you* can join the ranks of the 1 million plus people who successfully sell their house every year without using a real estate agent. Last one out, turn out the lights!

Appendix A

thevalueplay.com

Current ordering information for the FSBO Customizable Forms Kit, The Value Play Rental House Analyzer, Rehab Analyzer, Income Analyzer, Refi Analyzer, and other real estate products can be found at the Web site www.thevalueplay.com.

Other titles written by best-selling real estate author Steve Berges include:

The Complete Guide to Buying and Selling Apartment Buildings 2d Edition (New York: Wiley, 2004)

The Complete Guide to Flipping Properties (New York: Wiley, 2003)

The Complete Guide to Investing in Rental Properties (New York: McGraw-Hill, 2003)

101 Cost-Effective Ways to Improve the Value of Your Home (Chicago: Dearborn Trade, 2003)

The Complete Guide to Real Estate Finance for Investment Properties (New York: Wiley, 2004)

Appendix A

The Complete Guide to Investing in Undervalued Properties (New York: McGraw-Hill, 2005)

The Complete Guide to Investing in Foreclosures (New York: AMACOM, 2005)

Appendix B

symphony-homes.com

Symphony Homes is one of Michigan's premier builders of high-quality new homes. The company maintains a tradition of excellence by ensuring that each and every home built meets strict standards of quality. Symphony Homes is built on a foundation of three principals—quality, value, and service. From start to finish, the company takes care to ensure that only the best materials and the finest craftsmanship are utilized throughout the construction process. By partnering with key suppliers and efficiently managing our resources, we can effectively create value for home buyers by offering superior homes at competitive prices. Offering personal service to home buyers and fulfilling commitments to them allows members of the Symphony Homes team to provide each and every customer with an enjoyable building experience.

As a custom builder, Symphony Homes builds on home sites owned by individuals, or those owned by the company. New home construction services are offered in all of Genesee County, Lapeer County, and North Oakland County.

Appendix B

For information regarding Symphony Homes, one of Michigan's premier builders, please log on to the Web site www.symphony-homes.com.

Catch the Symphony Homes Vision!

Log on to www.symphony–homes.com!

Appendix C

Sample Real Estate Forms

Included in this section are samples of the 10 real estate forms for the seller, that were discussed in Chapter 5. These forms are available for immediate downloading in a PDF file format, as well as a fully customizable word-processing format at www.thevalueplay.com.

Ten FSBO Real Estate Forms

1. Residential Sales Contract
2. Property Condition Disclosure
3. Lead-Based Paint Disclosure
4. Third Party Financing Addendum
5. Loan Assumption Addendum
6. Seller Financing Addendum
7. Promissory Note
8. Notice of Termination
9. Warranty Deed
10. Quit Claim Deed

Appendix C

ONE TO FOUR FAMILY RESIDENTIAL CONTRACT (RESALE)

1. **PARTIES:** _____(Seller) agrees to sell and
convey to _____(Buyer) and Buyer agrees to
buy from Seller the Property described below.

2. **PROPERTY:**
A. LAND: Lot _____, Block _____, _____
County, State of Michigan, known as _____
(address/zip code), or as described on attached exhibit.
B. IMPROVEMENTS: The house, garage and all other fixtures and improvements attached
to the above-described real property, including without limitation, the following permanently
installed and built-in items, if any: all equipment and appliances, valances, screens, shutters,
awnings, wall-to-wall carpeting, mirrors, ceiling fans, attic fans, mail boxes, television antennas
and satellite dish system and equipment, heating and air-conditioning units, security and fire
detection equipment, wiring, plumbing and lighting fixtures, chandeliers, water softener system,
kitchen equipment, garage door openers, cleaning equipment, shrubbery, landscaping, outdoor
cooking equipment, and all other property owned by Seller and attached to the above described
real property.
C. ACCESSORIES: The following described related accessories, if any: window air
conditioning units, stove, fireplace screens, curtains and rods, blinds, window shades, draperies
and rods, controls for satellite dish system, controls for garage door openers, entry gate controls,
door keys, mailbox keys, above ground pool, swimming pool equipment and maintenance
accessories, and artificial fireplace logs.
D. EXCLUSIONS: The following improvements and accessories will be retained by
Seller and excluded:_____
_____
The land, improvements and accessories are collectively referred to as the "Property".

3. **SALES PRICE:**
A. Cash portion of Sales Price payable by Buyer at closing. . . . . $_____
B. Sum of all financing described below (excluding any loan funding
Fee or mortgage insurance premium). . . . . $_____
C. Sales Price (Sum of A and B). . . . . $_____

4. **FINANCING:** The portion of Sales Price not payable in cash will be paid as follows:
(Check applicable boxes below)

___ A. THIRD PARTY FINANCING: One or more third party mortgage loans in the total
amount of $_____. If the property does not satisfy the lenders' underwriting
requirements for the loan(s), this contract will terminate and the earnest money will be refunded
to Buyer. (Check one box only)
___(1) This contract is subject to Buyer being approved for the financing
described in the attached Third Party Financing Condition Addendum.
___(2) This contract is not subject to Buyer being approved for financing and does not
involve FHA or VA financing.
___B. ASSUMPTION: The assumption of the unpaid principal balance of one or more
promissory notes described in the attached TREC Loan Assumption Addendum.
___C. SELLER FINANCING: A promissory note from Buyer to Seller of $_____,
Bearing _____% interest per annum, secured by vendor's and deed of trust liens, and containing
the terms and conditions described in the attached TREC Seller Financing Addendum. If an
owner policy of title insurance is furnished, Buyer shall furnish Seller with a mortgagee policy of
title insurance.

5. **EARNEST MONEY:** Upon execution of this contract by both parties, Buyer shall deposit
$_____ as earnest money with _____, as
escrow agent, at _____(address). Buyer
shall deposit additional earnest money of $_____ with escrow agent within
_____ days after the effective date of this contract. If Buyer fails to deposit the earnest money as
required by this contract, Buyer will be in default.

Sample Real Estate Forms

6. **TITLE POLICY AND SURVEY:**
A. TITLE POLICY: Seller shall furnish to Buyer at ___Seller's ___Buyer's expense an owner policy of title insurance (Title Policy) issued by _____ _____(Title Company) in the amount of the Sales Price, dated at or after closing, insuring Buyer against loss under the provisions of the Title Policy, subject to the promulgated exclusions (including existing building and zoning ordinances) and the following exceptions:
(1) Restrictive convenants common to the platted subdivision in which the Property is located.
(2) The standard printed exception for standby fees, taxes and assessments.
(3) Liens created as part of the financing described in Paragraph 4.
(4) Utility easements created by the dedication deed or plat of the subdivision in which the Property is located.
(5) Reservations or exceptions otherwise permitted by this contract or as may be approved by Buyer in writing.
(6) The standard printed exception as to marital rights.
(7) The standard printed exception as to waters, tidelands, beaches, streams, and related matters.
(8) The standard printed exception as to discrepancies, conflicts, shortages in area or boundary lines, encroachments or protrusions, or overlapping improvements. Buyer, at Buyer's expense, may have the exception amended to read, "shortages in area".
B. COMMITMENT: Within 20 days after the Title Company receives a copy of this contract, Seller shall furnish to Buyer a commitment for title insurance (Commitment) and, at Buyer's expense, legible copies of restrictive covenants and documents evidencing exceptions in the Commitment (Exception Documents) other than the standard printed exceptions. Seller authorizes the Title Company to mail or hand deliver the Commitment and Exception Documents to Buyer at Buyer's address shown in Paragraph 21. If the Commitment and Exception Documents are not delivered to Buyer within the specified time, the time for delivery will be automatically extended up to 15 days or the Closing Date, whichever is earlier.
C. SURVEY: The survey must be made by a registered professional land surveyor acceptable to the Title Company and any lender. (Check one box only)
___(1) Within _____ days after the effective date of this contract, Seller, at Seller's expense, shall furnish a new survey to Buyer.
___(2) Within _____ days after the effective date of this contract, Buyer, at Buyer's expense, shall obtain a new survey.
___(3) Within _____ days after the effective date of this contract, Seller shall furnish Seller's existing survey of the Property to Buyer and the Title Company, along with Seller's affidavit acceptable to the Title Company for approval of the survey. If the survey is not approved by the Title Company or Buyer's lender, a new survey will be obtained at ___Seller's ___Buyer's expense no later than 3 days prior to the Closing Date.
D. OBJECTIONS: Within _____ days after Buyer receives the Commitment, Exception Documents and the survey, Buyer may object in writing to defects, exceptions, or encumbrances to title: disclosed on the survey other than items 6A(1) through (7) above; disclosed in the Commitment other than items 6A(1) through (8) above; or which prohibit the following use or activity:_____.
Buyer's failure to object within the time allowed will constitute a waiver of Buyer's right to object; except that the requirements in Schedule C of the Commitment are not waived. Seller shall cure the timely objections of Buyer or any third party lender within 15 days after Seller receives the objections and the Closing Date will be extended as necessary. If objections are not cured within such 15 day period, this contract will terminate and the earnest money will be refunded to Buyer unless Buyer waives the objections.
E. TITLE NOTICES:
(1)ABSTRACT OR TITLE POLICY: Broker advises Buyer to have an abstract of title covering the Property examined by an attorney of Buyer's selection, or Buyer should be furnished with or obtain a Title Policy. If a Title Policy is furnished, the Commitment should be promptly reviewed by an attorney of Buyer's choice due to the time limitations on Buyer's right to object.
(2)MANDATORY OWNERS' ASSOCIATION MEMBERSHIP: The Property ___is ___is not subject to mandatory membership in an owners' association. If the Property is subject to mandatory membership in an owners' association, Seller notifies Buyer under _____Michigan Property Code, that, as a purchaser of property in the residential community in which the Property is located, you are obligated to be a member of the owners' association. Restrictive convenants governing the use and occupancy of the Property and a dedicatory instrument governing the establishment, maintenance, and operation of this residential community have been or will be recorded in the Real Property Records of the county in which

Appendix C

the Property is located. Copies of the restrictive covenants and dedicatory instrument may be obtained from the county clerk. You are obligated to pay assessments to the owners' association. The amount of the assessments is subject to change. Your failure to pay the assessments could result in a lien on and the foreclosure of the Property.

(3)STATUTORY TAX DISTRICTS: If the Property is situated in a utility or other statutorily created district providing water, sewer, drainage, or flood control facilities and services, Chapter ____, Michigan Water Code requires Seller to deliver and Buyer to sign the statutory notice relating to the tax rate, bonded indebtedness, or standby fee of the district prior to final execution of this contract.

(4)TIDE WATERS: If the Property abuts the tidally influenced waters of the state, _____ Michigan Natural Resources Code, requires a notice regarding coastal area property to be included in the contract. An addendum containing the notice promulgated by TREC or required by the parties must be used.

(5)ANNEXATION: If the Property is located outside the limits of a municipality, Seller notifies Buyer under ____ Michigan Property Code, that the Property may now or later be included in the extraterritorial jurisdiction of a municipality and may now or later be subject to annexation by the municipality. Each municipality maintains a map that depicts its boundaries and extraterritorial jurisdiction. To determine if the Property is located within a municipality's extraterritorial jurisdiction or is likely to be located within a municipality's extraterritorial jurisdiction, contact all municipalities located in the general proximity of the Property for further information.

7.   **PROPERTY CONDITION:**

A. INSPECTIONS, ACCESS AND UTILITIES: Buyer may have the Property inspected by inspectors selected by Buyer and licensed to TREC or otherwise permitted by law to make inspections. Seller shall permit Buyer and Buyer's agents access to the Property at reasonable times. Seller shall pay for turning on existing utilities for inspections.

B. SELLER'S DISCLOSURE NOTICE PURSUANT TO ____, MICHIGAN PROPERTY CODE (Notice): (Check one box only)

___(1) Buyer has received the Notice.

___(2) Buyer has not received the Notice. Within ____ days after the effective date of this contract, Seller shall deliver the Notice to Buyer. If Buyer does not receive the Notice, Buyer may terminate this contract at any time prior to the closing and the earnest money will be refunded to Buyer. If Seller delivers the Notice, Buyer may terminate this contract for any reason within 7 days after Buyer receives the Notice or prior to the closing, whichever first occurs, and the earnest money will be refunded to Buyer.

___(3) The Michigan Property Code does not require this Seller to furnish the Notice.

C. SELLER'S DISCLOSURE OF LEAD-BASED PAINT AND LEAD-BASED PAINT HAZARDS is required by Federal law for a residential dwelling constructed prior to 1978.

D. ACCEPTANCE OF PROPERTY CONDITION: Buyer accepts the Property in its present condition; provided Seller, at Seller's expense, shall complete the following specific repairs and treatments:_____

_____

E. LENDER REQUIRED REPAIRS AND TREATMENTS: Unless otherwise agreed in writing, neither party is obligated to pay for lender required repairs, which includes treatment for wood destroying insects. If the parties do not agree to pay for the lender required repairs or treatments, this contract will terminate and the earnest money will be refunded to Buyer. If the cost of lender required repairs and treatments exceeds 5% of the Sales Price, Buyer may terminate this contract and the earnest money will be refunded to Buyer.

F. COMPLETION OF REPAIRS AND TREATMENTS: Unless otherwise agreed in writing, Seller shall complete all agreed repairs and treatments prior to the Closing Date. All required permits must be obtained, and repairs and treatments must be performed by persons who are licensed or otherwise authorized by law to provide such repairs or treatments. At Buyer's election, any transferable warranties received by Seller with respect to the repairs and treatments will be transferred to Buyer at Buyer's expense. If Seller fails to complete any agreed repairs and treatments prior to the Closing Date, Buyer may do so and receive reimbursement from Seller at closing. The Closing Date will be extended up to 15 days, if necessary, to complete repairs and treatments.

G. ENVIRONMENTAL MATTERS: Buyer is advised that the presence of wetlands, toxic substances, including asbestos and wastes or other environmental hazards, or the presence of a threatened or endangered species or its habitat may affect Buyer's intended use of the Property. If Buyer is concerned about these matters, an addendum promulgated by TREC or required by the parties should be used.

Sample Real Estate Forms

H. RESIDENTIAL SERVICE CONTRACTS: Buyer may purchase a residential service contract from a residential service company licensed by TREC. If Buyer purchases a residential service contract, Seller shall reimburse Buyer at closing for the cost of the residential service contract in an amount not exceeding $_____. Buyer should review any residential service contract for the scope of coverage, exclusions and limitations. **The purchase of a residential service contract is optional. Similar coverage may be purchased from various companies authorized to do business in Texas.**

8. **BROKERS' FEES:** All obligations of the parties for payment of brokers' fees are contained in separate written agreements.

9. **CLOSING:**
A. The closing of the sale will be on or before _____, 20___, or within 7 days after objections to matters disclosed in the Commitment or by the survey have been cured, whichever date is later (Closing Date). If either party fails to close the sale by the Closing Date, the non-defaulting party may exercise the remedies contained in Paragraph 15.
B. At closing:
(1) Seller shall execute and deliver a general warranty deed conveying title to the Property to Buyer and showing no additional exceptions to those permitted in Paragraph 6 and furnish tax statements or certificates showing no delinquent taxes on the Property.
(2) Buyer shall pay the Sales Price in good funds acceptable to the escrow agent.
(3) Seller and Buyer shall execute and deliver any notices, statements, certificates, affidavits, releases, loan documents and other documents required of them by this contract, the Commitment or law necessary for the closing of the sale and the issuance of the Title Policy.
C. Unless expressly prohibited by written agreement, Seller may continue to show the Property and receive, negotiate and accept back up offers.
D. All covenants, representations and warranties in this contract survive closing.

10. **POSSESSION:** Seller shall deliver to Buyer possession of the Property in its present or required condition, ordinary wear and tear excepted: ___upon closing and funding ___according to a temporary residential lease form promulgated by TREC or other written lease required by the parties. Any possession by Buyer prior to closing or by Seller after closing which is not authorized by a written lease will establish a tenancy at sufferance relationship between the parties. *Consult your insurance agent prior to change of ownership or possession because insurance coverage may be limited or terminated. The absence of a written lease or appropriate insurance coverage may expose the parties to economic loss.*

11. **SPECIAL PROVISIONS:**_____
_____
_____
_____

12. **SETTLEMENT AND OTHER EXPENSES:**
A. The following expenses must be paid at or prior to closing:
(1) Expenses payable by Seller (Seller's Expenses):
(a) Releases of existing liens, including prepayment penalties and recording fees; release of Seller's loan liability; tax statements or certificates; preparation of deed; one-half of escrow fee; and other expenses payable by Seller under this contract.
(b) Seller shall also pay an amount not to exceed $_____ to be applied in the following order: Buyer's Expenses which Buyer is prohibited from paying by FHA, VA, Texas Veteran's Housing Assistance Program or other governmental loan programs; Buyer's prepaid items; other Buyer's expenses.
(2) Expenses payable by Buyer (Buyer's Expenses):
(a) Loan origination, discount, buy-down, and commitment fees (Loan Fees).
(b) Appraisal fees; loan application fees; credit reports; preparation of loan documents; interest on the notes from date of disbursement to one month prior to dates of first monthly payments; recording fees; copies of easements and restrictions; mortgagee title policy with endorsements required by lender; loan-related inspection fees; photos, amortization schedules, one-half of escrow fee; all prepaid items, including required premiums for flood and hazard insurance, reserve deposits for insurance, ad valorem taxes and special governmental assessments; final compliance inspection; courier fee,

Appendix C

repair inspection, underwriting fee and wire transfer, expenses incident to any loan, and other expenses payable by Buyer under this contract.

B. Buyer shall pay Private Mortgage Insurance Premium (PMI), VA Loan Funding Fee, or FHA Mortgage Insurance Premium (MIP) as required by the lender

C. If any expense exceeds an amount expressly stated in this contract for such expense to be paid by a party, that party may terminate this contract unless the other party agrees to pay such excess. Buyer may not pay charges and fees expressly prohibited by FHA, VA, Texas Veteran's Housing Assistance Program or other governmental loan program regulations.

13. **PRORATIONS:** Taxes for the current year, interest, maintenance fees, assessments, dues and rents will be prorated through the Closing Date. If taxes for the current year vary from the amount prorated at closing, the parties shall adjust the prorations when tax statements for the current year are available. If taxes are not paid at or prior to closing, Buyer shall pay taxes for the current year.

14. **CASUALTY LOSS:** If any part of the Property is damaged or destroyed by fire or other casualty after the effective date of this contract, Seller shall restore the Property to its previous condition as soon as reasonable possible, but in any event by the Closing Date. If Seller fails to do so due to factors beyond Seller's control, Buyer may (a) terminate this contract and the earnest money will be refunded to Buyer (b) extend the time for performance up to 15 days and the Closing Date will be extended as necessary or (c) accept the Property in its damaged condition with an assignment of insurance proceeds and receive credit from Seller at closing in the amount of the deductible under the insurance policy. Seller's obligations under this paragraph are independent of any obligations of Seller under Paragraph 7.

15. **DEFAULT:** If Buyer fails to comply with this contract, Buyer will be in default, and Seller may (a) enforce specific performance, seek such other relief as may be provided by law, or both, or (b) terminate this contract and receive the earnest money as liquidated damages, thereby releasing both parties from this contract. If, due to factors beyond Seller's control, Seller fails within the time allowed to make any non-casualty repairs or deliver the Commitment, or survey, if required of Seller, Buyer may (a) extend the time for performance up to 15 days and the Closing Date will be extended as necessary or (b) terminate this contract as the sole remedy and receive the earnest money. If Seller fails to comply with this contract for any other reason, Seller will be in default and Buyer may (a) enforce specific performance, seek such other relief as may be provided by law, or both, or (b) terminate this contract and receive the earnest money thereby releasing both parties from this contract.

16. **MEDIATION:** It is the policy of the State of Texas to encourage resolution of disputes through alternative dispute resolution procedures such as mediation. Any dispute between Seller and Buyer related to this contract which is not resolved through informal discussion ___will ___will not be submitted to a mutually acceptable mediation service or provider. The parties to the mediation shall bear the mediation costs equally. This paragraph does not preclude a party from seeking equitable relief from a court of competent jurisdiction.

17. **ATTORNEY'S FEES:** The prevailing party in any legal proceeding related to this contract is entitled to recover reasonable attorney's fees and all costs of such proceeding incurred by the prevailing party.

18. **ESCROW:** The escrow agent is not (a) a party to this contract and does not have liability for the performance or nonperformance of any party to this contract, (b) liable for interest on the earnest money and (c) liable for the loss of any earnest money caused by the failure of any financial institution in which the earnest money has been deposited unless the financial institution is action as escrow agent. At closing, the earnest money must be applied first to any cash down payment, then to Buyer's Expenses and any excess refunded to Buyer. If both parties make written demand for the earnest money, escrow agent may require payment of unpaid expenses incurred on behalf of the parties and a written release of liability of escrow agent from all parties. If one party makes written demand for the earnest money, escrow agent shall give notice of the demand by providing to the other party a copy of the demand. If escrow agent does not receive written objection to the demand from the other party within 30 days after notice to the other party, escrow agent may disburse the earnest money to the party making demand reduced by the amount of unpaid expenses incurred on behalf of the party receiving the earnest money and escrow agent may pay the same to the creditors. If escrow agent complies with the provisions of this

paragraph, each party hereby releases escrow agent from all adverse claims related to the disbursal of the earnest money. Escrow agent's notice to the other party will be effective when deposited in the U.S. Mail, postage prepaid, certified mail, return receipt requested, addressed to the other party at such party's address shown below. Notice of objection to the demand will be deemed effective upon receipt by escrow agent.

19. **REPRESENTATIONS:** Seller represents that as of the Closing Date (a) there will be no liens, assessments, or security interests against the Property which will not be satisfied out of the sales proceeds unless securing payment of any loans assumed by Buyer and (b) assumed loans will not be in default. If any representation of Seller in this contract is untrue on the Closing Date, Buyer may terminate this contract and the earnest money will be refunded to Buyer.

20. **FEDERAL TAX REQUIREMENTS:** If Seller is a "foreign person," as defined by applicable law, or if Seller fails to deliver an affidavit to Buyer that Seller is not a "foreign person," then Buyer shall withhold from the sales proceeds an amount sufficient to comply with applicable tax law and deliver the same to the Internal Revenue Service together with appropriate tax forms. Internal Revenue Service regulations require filing written reports if currency in excess of specified amounts is received in the transaction.

21. **AGREEMENT OF PARTIES:** This contract contains the entire agreement of the parties and cannot be changed except by their written agreement.

22. **CONSULT AN ATTORNEY:** Real estate licensees cannot give legal advice. READ THIS CONTRACT CAREFULLY. If you do not understand the effect of the contract, consult an attorney BEFORE signing.

Buyer's   Seller's
Attorney is: _____   Attorney is: _____

_____   _____

Telephone: (___)_____   _____

Facsimile: (___)_____   _____

EXECUTED the _____ day of _____, 20___ (EFFECTIVE DATE).
(BROKER: FILL IN THE DATE OF FINAL ACCEPTANCE.)

_____   _____
Buyer   Seller

_____   _____
Buyer   Seller

Appendix C

SELLER'S DISCLOSURE OF PROPERTY CONDITION

CONCERNING THE PROPERTY AT _____
(Street Address and City)

THIS NOTICE IS A DISCLOSURE OF SELLER'S KNOWLEDGE OF THE CONDITION OF THE PROPERTY AS OF THE DATE SIGNED BY SELLER AND IS NOT A SUBSTITUTE FOR ANY INSPECTIONS OR WARRANTIES THE PURCHASER MAY WISH TO OBTAIN. IT IS NOT A WARRANTY OF ANY KIND BY SELLER OR SELLER'S AGENTS.

Seller _____ is _____ is not occupying the Property. If unoccupied, how long since Seller has occupied the Property?

_____

1. The Property has the items checked below. [Write Yes (Y), No (N), or Unknown (U)]:

___ Range	___ Oven	___ Microwave
___ Dishwasher	___ Trash Compactor	___ Disposal
___ Washer/Dryer Hookups	___ Window Screens	___ Rain Gutters
___ Security System	___ Fire Detection Equipment	___ Intercom System
___ TV Antenna	___ Cable TV Wiring	___ Satellite Dish
___ Ceiling Fan(s)	___ Attic Fan(s)	___ Exhaust Fan(s)
___ Central A/C	___ Central Heating	___ Wall/Window A/C
___ Plumbing System	___ Septic System	___ Public Sewer System
___ Patio/Decking	___ Outdoor Grill	___ Fences
___ Pool	___ Sauna	___ Spa ___ Hot Tub
___ Pool Equipment	___ Pool Heater	___ Automatic Lawn Sprinkler System

___ Fireplace(s) & Chimney (Woodburning) ___ Fireplace(s) & Chimney (Mock) ___ Gas Lines (Nat./LP)
___ Gas Fixtures   Garage: ___ Attached   ___ Carport
                              ___ Not Attached
Garage Door Opener(s):   ___ Electronic   ___ Control(s)
Water Heater: ___ Gas   ___ Electric
Water Supply: ___ City   ___ Well   ___ MUD   ___ Co-op

Roof Type: _____   Age: _____ (approx)

Are you (Seller) aware of any of the above items that are not in working condition, that have known defects, or that are in need of repair? ___ Yes ___ No ___ Unknown. If yes, then describe. (Attach additional sheets if necessary):

_____

_____

2. Are you (Seller) aware of any known defects/malfunctions in any of the following? Write Yes (Y) if you are aware, write No (N) if you are not aware.

___ Interior Walls	___ Ceilings	___ Floors
___ Exterior Walls	___ Doors	___ Windows
___ Roof	___ Foundation/ Slab(s)	___ Basement
___ Walls/Fences	___ Driveways	___ Sidewalks
___ Plumbing/ Sewers/ Septics	___ Electrical Systems	___ Lighting Fixtures

Other Structural Components (Describe)_____

_____

If the answer to any of the above is yes, explain. (Attach additional sheets if necessary):

_____

_____

Sample Real Estate Forms

3. Are you (Seller) aware of any of the following conditions? Write Yes (Y) if you are aware, write No (N) if you are not aware.

___ Active Termites (includes wood-Destroying insects)
___ Termite or Wood Rot Damage Needing Repair
___ Previous Termite Damage

___ Previous Termite Treatment
___ Previous Flooding
___ Improper Drainage

___ Water Penetration
___ Located in 100-Year Floodplain
___ Present Flood Insurance Coverage

___ Previous Structural or Roof Repair
___ Hazardous or Toxic Waste
___ Asbestos Components

___ Urea-formaldehyde Insulation
___ Radon Gas
___ Lead Based Paint

___ Aluminum Wiring
___ Previous Fires
___ Unplatted Easements

___ Landfill, Settling, Soil Movement, Fault Lines
___ Subsurface Structure or Pits

If the answer to any of the above is yes, explain. (Attach additional sheets if necessary):

_____

_____

4. Are you (Seller) aware of any item, equipment, or system in or on the Property that is in need of repair? ___ Yes (if you are aware) ___ No (if you are not aware). If yes, explain (attach additional sheets as necessary).

_____

_____

5. Are you (Seller) aware of any of the following? Write Yes (Y) if you are aware, write No (N) if you are not aware.

___ Room additions, structural modifications, or other alterations or repairs made without necessary permits or not in compliance with building codes in effect at that time.

___ Homeowners' Association or maintenance fees or assessments.

___ Any "common area" (facilities such as pools, tennis courts, walkways, or other areas) co-owned in undivided interest with others.

___ Any notices of violations of deed restrictions or governmental ordinances affecting the condition or use of the Property.

___ Any lawsuits directly or indirectly affecting the Property.

___ Any condition on the Property which materially affects the physical health or safety of an individual.

If the answer to any of the above is yes, explain. (Attach additional sheets if necessary): _____

_____

_____

_____   _____
Date   Signature of Seller   Date   Signature of Seller

The undersigned purchaser hereby acknowledges receipt of the foregoing notice.

_____   _____
Date   Signature of Seller   Date   Signature of Seller

Appendix C

DISCLOSURE OF INFORMATION AND ACKNOWLEDGMENT OF LEAD-BASED PAINT AND/OR LEAD-BASED PAINT HAZARDS

Our Home At _____ Was Built In: _____ Dated: _____

Seller: _____ Seller: _____

Lead Warning Statement:

Every purchaser of any interest in residential real property on which a residential dwelling was built prior to 1978 in notified that such property might present exposure to lead from lead-based paint that may place young children at risk of developing lead poisoning. Lead poisoning in young children may produce permanent neurological damage, including learning disabilities, reduced intelligence quotient, behavioral problems, and impaired memory. Lead poisoning also poses a particular risk to pregnant women. The seller of any interest in residential real property is required to provide the buyer with any information on lead-based paint hazards. A risk assessment or inspection for possible lead-based paint hazards is recommended prior to purchase.

NOTE: IF THE HOUSING BEING LISTED OR SOLD WAS BUILT IN 1978 OR AFTER – YOU _DO NOT_ HAVE TO FILL OUT THE REMAINDER OF THIS FORM.

Seller's Disclosure (initial)

_____ (A) Presence of lead-based paint and/or lead-based paint hazards (check one below):
   [ ] Known lead-based paint and/or lead-based paint hazards are present in the housing
   (Explain)_____
   _____

   [ ] Seller has no knowledge of lead-based paint and/or lead-based paint hazards in the housing.

_____ (B) Records and Reports available to the seller (check one below):
   [ ] Seller has provided the purchaser with all available records and reports pertaining to lead-based paint and/or lead-base hazards in the housing (list documents below):
   _____
   _____

   [ ] Seller has no reports or records pertaining to lead-based paint and/or lead-based paint hazards in the housing.

Purchaser's Acknowledgement (initial)

_____ (C) Purchaser has received copies of all information listed above.

_____ (D) Purchaser has received the pamphlet _Protect Your Family From Lead In Your Home._

_____ (E) Purchaser has (check one below):
      [ ] Received a 10-day opportunity (or mutually agreed upon period) to conduct a risk assessment or inspection of the presence of lead-based paint or lead-based paint hazards, or...
      [ ] Waived the opportunity to conduct a risk assessment for the presence of lead-based and or lead-based paint hazards.

Agent's Acknowledgement (initial)

_____ (F) Agent has informed the seller of the seller's obligations under 42 U.S.C. 4852 d and is aware of his/her responsibilities to ensure compliance.

Certification of Accuracy

The following parties have reviewed the information above and certify, to the best of their knowledge, that the information they have provided is true and accurate.

Seller: _____ Date: _____ Purchaser: _____ Date: _____

Seller: _____ Date: _____ Purchaser: _____ Date: _____

Agent: _____ Date: _____ Agent: _____ Date: _____

Note: Intact lead-based paint that is in good condition is not necessarily a hazard. See EPA pamphlet _Protect Your Family From Lead In Your Home_ for more information.

THIRD PARTY FINANCING CONDITION ADDENDUM

TO CONTRACT CONCERNING THE PROPERTY AT

_____

(Street Address and City)

Buyer shall apply promptly for all financing described below and make every reasonable effort to obtain financing approval. Financing approval will be deemed to have been obtained when the lender determines that Buyer has satisfied all of lender's financial requirements (those items relating to Buyer's assets, income and credit history). If financing (including any financed PMI premium) approval is not obtained within _____ days after the effective date, this contract will terminate and the earnest money will be refunded to Buyer. Each note must be secured by vendor's and deed of trust liens.

CHECK APPLICABLE BOXES:

___ A. CONVENTIONAL FINANCING:
    ___ (1) A first mortgage loan in the principal amount of $_____ (excluding any financed PMI premium), due in full in _____ year(s), with interest not to exceed _____% per annum for the first _____ year(s) of the loan with Loan Fees not to exceed _____ % of the loan. The loan will be ___ with ___ without PMI.
    ___ (2) A second mortgage loan in the principal amount of $_____ (excluding any financed PMI premium), due in full in _____ year(s), with interest not to exceed _____% per annum for the first _____ year(s) of the loan with Loan Fees not to exceed _____ % of the loan. The loan will be ___ with ___ without PMI.

___ B. TEXAS VETERANS' HOUSING ASSISTANCE PROGRAM LOAN: A Texas Veteran's Housing Assistance Program Loan of $_____ for a period of at least _____ years at the interest rate established by the Texas Veteran's Land Board at the time of closing.

___ C. FHA INSURED FINANCING: A Section _____ FHA insured loan of not less than $_____ (excluding any financed MIP), amortizable monthly for not less than _____ years, with interest not to exceed _____ % per annum for the first _____ year(s) of the loan with Loan Fees not to exceed _____ % of the loan. As required by HUD-FHA, if FHA valuation is unknown, *"It is expressly agreed that, notwithstanding any other provision of this contract, the purchaser (Buyer) shall not be obligated to complete the purchase of the Property described herein or to incur any penalty by forfeiture of earnest money deposits or otherwise unless the purchaser (Buyer) has been given in accordance with HUD/FHA or VA requirements a written statement issued by the Federal Housing Commissioner, Department of Veterans Affairs, or a Direct Endorsement Lender setting forth the appraised value of the Property of not less than $_____. The purchaser (Buyer) shall have the privilege and option of proceeding with consummation of the contract without regard to the amount of the appraised valuation. The appraised valuation is arrived at to determine the maximum mortgage the Department of Housing and Urban Development will insure. HUD does not warrant the value or the condition of the Property. The purchaser (Buyer) should satisfy himself/herself that the price and the condition of the Property are acceptable."*

If the FHA appraised value of the Property (excluding closing costs and MIP) is less than the Sales Price, Seller may reduce the Sales Price to an amount equal to the FHA appraised value (excluding closing costs and MIP) and the sale will be closed at the lower Sales Price with proportionate adjustments to the down payment and loan amount.

___ D. VA GUARANTEED FINANCING: A VA guaranteed loan of not less than $_____ (excluding any financed Funding Fee), amortizable monthly for not less than _____ years, with interest not to exceed _____ % per annum for the first _____ year(s) of the loan with Loan Fees not to exceed _____ % of the loan.

Appendix C

VA NOTICE TO BUYER: *"It is expressly agreed that, notwithstanding any other provisions of this contract, the Buyer shall not incur any penalty by forfeiture of earnest money or otherwise or be obligated to complete the purchase of the Property described herein, if the contract purchase price or cost exceeds the reasonable value of the Property established by the Department of Veterans Affairs. The Buyer shall, however, have the privilege and option of proceeding with the consummation of this contract without regard to the amount of the reasonable value established by the Department of Veterans Affairs."*

If Buyer elects to complete the purchase at an amount in excess of the reasonable value established by VA, Buyer shall pay such excess amount in cash from a source which Buyer agrees to disclose to the VA and which Buyer represents will not be from borrowed funds except as approved by VA. If VA reasonable value of the Property is less than the Sales Price, Seller may reduce the Sales Price to an amount equal to the VA reasonable value and the sale will be closed at the lower Sales Price with proportionate adjustments to the down payment and the loan amount.

_____   _____
Buyer   Seller

_____   _____
Buyer   Seller

Sample Real Estate Forms

LOAN ASSUMPTION ADDENDUM
TO CONTRACT CONCERNING THE PROPERTY AT

_____
(Street Address and City)

A. **CREDIT DOCUMENTATION.** Within _____ days after the effective date of this contract, Buyer shall deliver to Seller ___ credit report ___ verification of employment, including salary ___ verification of funds on deposit in financial institutions ___ current financial statements to establish Buyer's creditworthiness and ___ _____.

Buyer hereby authorizes any credit reporting agency to furnish to Seller at Buyer's sole expense copies of Buyer's credit reports.

B. **CREDIT APPROVAL.** If Buyer's documentation is not delivered within the specified time, Seller may terminate this contract by notice to Buyer within 7 days after expiration of the time for delivery, and the earnest money will be paid to Seller. If the documentation is timely delivered, and Seller determines in Seller's sole discretion that Buyer's credit is unacceptable, Seller may terminate this contract by notice to Buyer within 7 days after expiration of the time for delivery and the earnest money will be refunded to Buyer. If Seller does not terminate this contract, Seller will be deemed to have accepted Buyer's credit.

C. **ASSUMPTION.**

___(1) The unpaid principal balance of a first lien promissory note payable to _____ _____ which unpaid balance at closing will be $_____. The total current monthly payment including principal, interest and any reserve deposits is $_____. Buyer's initial payment will be the first payment due after closing.

___(2) The unpaid principal balance of a second lien promissory note payable to _____ _____ which unpaid balance at closing will be $_____. The total current monthly payment including principal, interest and any reserve deposits is $_____. Buyer's initial payment will be the first payment due after closing.

Buyer's assumption of an existing note includes all obligations imposed by the deed of trust securing the note. If the unpaid principal balance(s) of any assumed loan(s) as of the Closing Date varies from the loan balance(s) stated above, the ___ cash payable at closing ___ Sales Price will be adjusted by the amount of any variance; provided, if the total principal balance of all assumed loans varies in an amount greater than $350.00 at closing, either party may terminate this contract and the earnest money will be refunded to Buyer unless the other party elects to eliminate the excess in the variance by an appropriate adjustment at closing. Buyer may terminate this contract and the earnest money will be refunded to Buyer if the noteholder requires (a) payment of an assumption fee in excess of $_____ in (1) above or $_____ in (2) above and Seller declines to pay such excess, (b) an increase in the interest rate to more than _____% in (1) above, or _____% in (2) above, (c) any other modification of the loan documents, or (d) consent to the assumption of the loan and fails to consent. A vendor's lien and deed of trust to secure assumption will be required which will automatically be released on execution and delivery of a release by noteholder. If Seller is released from liability on any assumed note, the vendor's lien and deed of trust to secure assumption will not be required. If noteholder maintains an escrow account, the escrow account must be transferred to Buyer without any deficiency. Buyer shall reimburse Seller for the amount in the transferred accounts.

NOTICE TO BUYER: The monthly payments, interest rates or other terms of some loans may be adjusted by the noteholder at or after closing. If you are concerned about the possibility of future adjustments, do not sign the contract without examining the notes and deeds of trust.

NOTICE TO SELLER: Your liability to pay the note assumed by Buyer will continue unless you obtain a release of liability from the noteholder. If you are concerned about future liability, you should use the TREC Release of Liability Addendum.

_____   _____
Buyer   Seller

_____   _____
Buyer   Seller

Appendix C

SELLER FINANCING ADDENDUM
TO CONTRACT CONCERNING THE PROPERTY AT

_____

(Street Address and City)

A. CREDIT DOCUMENTATION Within _____ days after the effective date of this contract, Buyer shall deliver to Seller ____ credit report ___ verification of employment, including salary ____ verification of funds on deposit in financial institutions ____ current financial statement to establish Buyer's creditworthiness. Buyer hereby authorizes any credit reporting agency to furnish to Seller at Buyer's sole expense copies of Buyer's credit reports.

B. CREDIT APPROVAL If Buyer's documentation is not delivered within the specified time, Seller may terminate this contract by notice to Buyer within 7 days after expiration of the time for delivery, and the earnest money will be paid to Seller. If the documentation is timely delivered, and Seller determines in Seller's sole discretion that Buyer's credit is unacceptable, Seller may terminate this contract by notice to Buyer within 7 days after expiration of the time for delivery and the earnest money will be refunded to Buyer. If Seller does not terminate this contract, Seller will be deemed to have accepted Buyer's credit.

C. PROMISSORY NOTE The promissory note (Note) described in Paragraph 4 of this contract payable by Buyer to the order of Seller will be payable at the place designated by Seller. Buyer may prepay the Note in whole or in part at any time without penalty. Any prepayments are to be applied to the payment of the installments of principal last maturing and interest will immediately cease on the prepaid principal. The Note will contain a provision for payment of a late fee of 5% of any installment not paid within 10 days of the due date. The Note will be payable as follows:
___(1) In one payment due _____ after the date of the Note with interest payable _____.
___(2) In _____ installments of $_____ including interest ___ plus interest beginning _____ after the date of the note and continuing at _____ intervals thereafter for _____ when the balance of the note will be due and payable.
___(3) Interest only in _____ installments for the first _____ month(s) and thereafter in installments of $_____ including interest ___ plus interest beginning _____ after the date of the Note and continuing at _____ intervals thereafter for _____ when the balance of the Note will be due and payable.

D. DEED OF TRUST The deed of trust securing the Note will provide for the following:
(1) PROPERTY TRANSFERS: (check only one)
___ (a) Consent Not Required: The Property may be sold, conveyed or leased without the consent of Seller, provided any subsequent buyer assumes the Note.
___ (b) Consent Required: If all or any part of the Property is sold, conveyed, leased for a period longer than 3 years, leased with an option to purchase, or otherwise sold (including any contract for deed), without the prior written consent of Seller, Seller may declare the balance of the Note, to be immediately due and payable. The creation of a subordinate lien, any conveyance under threat or order of condemnation, any deed solely between buyers, the passage of title by reason of the death of a buyer or by operation of law will not entitle Seller to exercise the remedies provided in this paragraph.
(1) TAX AND INSURANCE ESCROW: (check only one)
___(a) Escrow Not Required: Buyer shall furnish Seller annually, before the taxes become delinquent, evidence that all taxes on the Property have been paid. Buyer shall furnish Seller annually evidence of paid-up casualty insurance naming Seller as an additional loss payee.
___(b) Escrow Required: With each installment Buyer shall deposit with Seller in escrow a pro rata part of the estimated annual ad valorem taxes and casualty insurance premiums for the Property. Buyer shall pay any deficiency within 30 days after notice from Seller. Buyer's failure to pay the deficiency constitutes a default under the deed of trust. Buyer is not required to deposit any escrow payments for taxes and insurance that are deposited with a superior lienholder. The casualty insurance must name Seller as an additional loss payee.
(3) PRIOR LIENS: Any default under any lien superior to the lien securing the Note constitutes default under the deed of trust securing the Note.

_____   _____
Buyer   Seller

_____   _____
Buyer   Seller

Sample Real Estate Forms

PROMISSORY NOTE

Principal	Loan Date	Maturity Date	Loan No	Account	Officer

References in the shaded area are for Lender's use only and do not limit the applicability of this document to any particular loan or item. Any item above containing "***" has been omitted due to text length limitations.

Borrower: Lender:

Principal Amount: _____   Initial Rate: _____   Date of Note: _____
Monthly Payment: _____

PROMISE TO PAY. _____ ("Borrower:) promises to pay to _____ ("Lender"), or order, in lawful Money of the United States of America, the principal amount of _____ Dollars ($_____) or so much as may be outstanding, together with interest on the unpaid outstanding principal balance of each advance. Interest shall be calculated from the date of each advance until repayment of each advance. The interest rate will not increase above _____%.

PAYMENT. Borrower will pay this loan in one payment of all outstanding principal plus all accrued unpaid interest on _____. In addition, Borrower will pay regular monthly payments of all accrued unpaid interest in the amount of $_____ due as of each payment date, beginning _____, with all subsequent interest payments to be due on the same day of each month after that. Unless otherwise agreed or required by applicable law, payments will be applied first to accrued unpaid interest, then to principal, and any remaining amount to any unpaid collection costs and late charges. The annual interest rate for this Note is computed on a 365/360 basis; that is, by applying the ratio of the annual interest rate over a year of 360 days, multiplied by the outstanding principal balance, multiplied by the actual number of days the principal balance is outstanding. Borrower will pay Lender at Lender's address shown above or at such other place as Lender may designate in writing.

PREPAYMENT. Borrower may pay without penalty all or a portion of the amount owed earlier than it is due. Early payments will not, unless agreed to by Lender in writing, relieve Borrower of Borrower's obligation to continue to make payments of accrued unpaid interest. Rather, early payments will reduce the principal balance due. Borrower agrees not to send Lender payments marked "paid in full", "without recourse", or similar language. If Borrower sends such a payment, Lender may accept it without losing any of Lender's rights under this Note, and Borrower will remain obligated to pay any further amount owed to Lender. All written communications concerning disputed amounts, including any check or other payment instrument that indicates that the payment constitutes "payment in full" of the amount owed or that is tendered with other conditions or limitations or as full satisfaction of a disputed amount, must be mailed or delivered to the following address: _____

LATE CHARGE. If a payment is 3 days or more late, Borrower will be charged $_____.

INTEREST AFTER DEFAULT. Upon default, including failure to pay upon final maturity, Lender, at its option, may, if permitted under applicable law, increase the variable interest rate on this Note to _____% per annum. The interest rate will not exceed the maximum rate permitted by applicable law.

DEFAULT. Each of the following shall constitute an event of default ("Event of Default") under this Note:

    Payment Default. Borrower fails to make any payments when due under this Note.

    Other Defaults. Borrower fails to comply with or to perform any other term, obligation, covenant or condition contained in this Note or in any of the related documents or to comply with or to perform any term, obligation, covenant or condition contained in any other agreement between Lender and Borrower.

    False Statements. Any warranty, representation or statement made or furnished to Lender by Borrower or on Borrower's behalf under this Note or the related documents is false or misleading in any material respect, either now or at the time made or furnished or becomes false or misleading at any time thereafter.

    Death or Insolvency. The dissolution of Borrower (regardless of whether election to continue is made), any member withdraws from Borrower, or any other termination of Borrower's existence as a going business or the death of any member, the insolvency of Borrower, the appointment of a receiver for any part of Borrower's property, any assignment for the benefit of creditors, any type of creditor workout, or the commencement of any proceeding under any bankruptcy or insolvency laws by or against Borrower.

    Creditor or Forfeiture Proceedings. Commencement of foreclosure or forfeiture proceedings, whether by judicial proceeding, self-help, repossession or any other method, by any creditor of Borrower or by any governmental agency against any collateral securing the loan. This includes a garnishment of any of Borrower's accounts, including deposit accounts, with Lender. However, this Event of Default shall not apply if there is a good faith dispute by Borrower as to the validity or reasonableness of the claim which is the basis of the creditor or forfeiture proceeding and if Borrower gives Lender written notice of the creditor or forfeiture proceeding and deposits with Lender monies or forfeiture proceeding, in an amount determined by Lender, in its sole discretion, as being an adequate reserve or bond for the dispute.

    Events Affection Guarantor. Any of the preceding events occurs with respect to any Guarantor of any of the indebtedness or any Guarantor dies or becomes incompetent, or revokes or disputes the validity of, or liability under, any guaranty of the indebtedness evidenced by this Note.

    Adverse Change. A material adverse change occurs in Borrower's financial condition, or Lender believes the prospect of payment or performance of this Note is impaired.

Appendix C

Insecurity. Lender in good faith believes itself insecure.

LENDER'S RIGHTS. Upon default, Lender may declare the entire unpaid principal balance on this Note and all accrued unpaid interest immediately due, and then Borrower will pay that amount.

ATTORNEYS' FEES; EXPENSES. Lender may hire or pay someone else to help collect this Note if Borrower does not pay. Borrower will pay Lender that amount. This includes, subject to any limits under applicable law, Lender's reasonable attorneys' fees and Lender's legal expenses whether or not there is a lawsuit, including reasonable attorneys' fees and expenses for bankruptcy proceedings (including efforts to modify or vacate any automatic stay or injunction), and appeals. If not prohibited by applicable law, Borrower also will pay any court costs, in addition to all other sums provided by law.

JURY WAIVER. Lender and Borrower hereby waive the right to any jury trial in any action, proceeding, or counterclaim brought by either Lender or Borrower against the other.

GOVERNING LAW. This Note will be governed by, construed and enforced in accordance with federal law and the laws of the State of Michigan. This Note has been accepted by Lender in the State of Michigan.

RIGHT OF SETOFF. To the extent permitted by applicable law, Lender reserves a right of setoff in all Borrower's accounts with Lender (whether checking, savings, or some other account). This includes all accounts Borrower holds jointly with someone else and all accounts Borrower may open in the future. However, this does not include any IRA or Keogh accounts, or any trust accounts for which setoff would be prohibited by law. Borrower authorizes Lender, to the extent permitted by applicable law, to charge or setoff all sums owing on the indebtedness against any and all such accounts, and, at Lender's option, to administratively freeze all such accounts to allow Lender to protect Lender's charge and setoff rights provided in this paragraph.

COLLATERAL. Borrower acknowledges this Note is secured by a _____.

SUCCESSOR INTERESTS. The terms of this Note shall be binding upon Borrower, and upon Borrower's heirs, personal representatives, successors and assigns, and shall inure to the benefit of Lender and its successors and assigns.

NOTIFY US OF INACCURATE INFORMATION WE REPORT TO CONSUMER REPORTING AGENCIES. Please notify us if we report any inaccurate information about your account(s) to a consumer reporting agency. Your written notice describing the specific inaccuracy(ies) should be sent to us at the following address: _____.

GENERAL PROVISIONS. Lender may delay or forgo enforcing any of its rights or remedies under this Note without losing them. Borrower and any other person who signs, guarantees or endorses this Note, to the extent allowed by law, waive presentment, demand for payment, and notice of dishonor. Upon any change in the terms of this Note, and unless otherwise expressly stated in writing to party who signs this Note, whether as maker, guarantor, accommodation maker or endorser, shall be released from liability. All such parties agree that Lender may renew or extend (repeatedly and for any length of time) this loan or release any party or guarantor or collateral; or impair, fail to realize upon or perfect Lender's security interest in the collateral; and take any other action deemed necessary by Lender without the consent of or notice to anyone. All such parties also agree that Lender may modify this loan without the consent of or notice to anyone other than the party with whom the modification is made. The obligations under this Note are joint and several.

PRIOR TO SIGNING THIS NOTE, BORROWER READ AND UNDERSTOOD ALL THE PROVISIONS OF THIS NOTE. BORROWER AGREES TO THE TERMS OF THE NOTE.

BORROWER ACKNOWLEDGES RECEIPT OF A COMPLETED COPY OF THIS PROMISSORY NOTE.

BORROWER:

By:_____   By:_____

Date: _____   Date: _____

WITNESS:

By: _____

Date: _____

NOTICE OF TERMINATION OF CONTRACT

To: Seller(s)

In accordance with the unrestricted right of Buyer to terminate the contract between

_____

As Seller and _____

As Buyer dated _____, 20_____ for the Property located at _____

_____

Buyer notifies Seller that the contract is terminated.

_____   _____
Buyer   Date   Buyer   Date

Appendix C

WARRANTY DEED

KNOW ALL MEN BY THESE PRESENTS: That _____, whose address is

_____

Convey(s) and Warrant(s) to _____

Whose address is _____

The following described premises situated in _____, County of

_____ and State of _____.

for the full consideration of $_____ subject to all building and use restrictions and

easements, if any, of record.


```
 ---------------------------------------
              (Name)
```


```
 ---------------------------------------
            (Signature)
```

STATE OF _____ }

COUNTY OF _____   }

The foregoing instrument was acknowledged before me this _____ day of _____, 20____ by

_____ of _____, on behalf of the said

Corporation.

_____
(Notary Public)

Prepared by: _____

When recorded return to: _____

Sample Real Estate Forms

QUIT CLAIM DEED

KNOW ALL MEN BY THESE PRESENTS: That _____,

whose address is _____

Quit Claim(s) to _____ whose address is _____

_____

The following described premises situated in _____, County of _____

and State of Michigan.

Together with all and singular the tenements, hereditaments and appurtenances thereunto belonging or in anywise

appertaining, for the sum of _____.

Exemptions:

Dated: _____

_____
(Name)

_____
(Signature)

STATE OF _____ }
                                  }   ss   _____
COUNTY OF _____ }   (Signature)

The foregoing instrument was acknowledged before me this _____ day of _____, 20___

by _____, and _____ of _____

_____, on behalf of the said Corporation.

_____
Notary Public

Prepared by: _____

When recorded return to: _____

Glossary

Real estate investors will find the Glossary helpful for understanding words and terms used in real estate transactions. There are, however, some factors that may affect these definitions. Terms are defined as they are commonly understood in the mortgage and real estate industry. The same terms may have different meanings in another context. The definitions are intentionally general, nontechnical, and short. They do not encompass all possible meanings or nuances that a term may acquire in legal use. State laws, as well as custom and use in various states or regions of the country, may, in fact, modify or completely change the meanings of certain terms defined. Before signing any documents or depositing any money preparatory to entering into a real estate contract, the purchaser should consult with an attorney of his or her choice to ensure that his or her rights are properly protected.

Abstract of Title A summary of the public records relating to the title for a particular piece of land. An attorney or title insurance company reviews an abstract of title to determine whether there are any title defects that must be cleared before a buyer can purchase clear, marketable, and insurable title.

Glossary

Acceleration Clause Condition in a mortgage that may require the balance of the loan to become due immediately in the event regular mortgage payments are not made or for breach of other conditions of the mortgage.

Adjustable Rate Mortgage Loans (ARM) Loans with interest rates that are adjusted periodically based on changes in a preselected index. As a result, the interest rate on your loan and the monthly payment will rise and fall with increases and decreases in overall interest rates. These mortgage loans must specify how their interest rate changes, usually in terms of a relation to a national index such as (but not always) Treasury bill rates. If interest rates rise, your monthly payments will rise. An interest rate cap limits the amount by which the interest rate can change; look for this feature when you consider an ARM loan.

Ad Valorem Designates an assessment of taxes against property in a literal sense according to its value.

Adverse Possession A possession that is inconsistent with the right of possession and the title of the true owner. It is the actual, open, notorious, exclusive, continuous, and hostile occupation and possession of the land of another under a claim of right or under color of title.

Affidavit Written statement made under oath before an officer of the court or notary public.

Agency The relationship that exists by contract whereby one person is authorized to represent and act on behalf of another person in various business transactions.

Agreement of Sale Known by various names, such as contract of purchase, purchase agreement, or sales agreement according to location or jurisdiction. A contract in which a seller agrees to sell and a buyer agrees to buy, under certain specific terms and conditions spelled out in writing and signed by both parties.

Amortization A payment plan that enables the borrower to reduce a debt gradually through monthly payments of principal, thereby liquidating or extinguishing the obligation through a series of installments.

Appraisal Expert judgment or estimate of the quality or value of real estate as of a given date. The process through which conclusions of property value are obtained. It also refers to the formalized report that sets forth the estimate and conclusion of value.

Assessed Value An official valuation of property most often used for tax purposes.

Assignment The method or manner by which a right, a specialty, or a contract is transferred from one person to another.

Glossary

Assumption of Mortgage An obligation undertaken by the purchaser of property to be personally liable for payment of an existing mortgage. In an assumption, the purchaser is substituted for the original mortgagor in the mortgage instrument and the original mortgagor is to be released from further liability in the assumption. The mortgagee's consent is usually required. The original mortgagor should always obtain a written release from further liability if he desires to be fully released under the assumption. Failure to obtain such a release renders the original mortgagor liable if the person assuming the mortgage fails to make the monthly payments. An assumption of mortgage is often confused with "purchasing subject to a mortgage." When one purchases subject to a mortgage, the purchaser agrees to make the monthly mortgage payments on an existing mortgage, but the original mortgagor remains personally liable if the purchaser fails to make the monthly payments. Since the original mortgagor remains liable in the event of default, the mortgagee's consent is not required for a sale subject to a mortgage. Both assumption of mortgage and purchasing subject to a mortgage are used to finance the sale of property. They may also be used when a mortgagor is in financial difficulty and desires to sell the property to avoid foreclosure.

Automatic Stay A bankruptcy provision that stops any act that can be construed to be an act against the interests of the debtor or the debtor's property.

Bankruptcy A proceeding in a federal court to relieve certain debts of a person or a business unable to pay its debts.

Binder or Offer to Purchase A preliminary agreement, secured by the payment of earnest money, between a buyer and seller as an offer to purchase real estate. A binder secures the right to purchase real estate on agreed-upon terms for a limited period of time. If the buyer changes her mind or is unable to purchase, the earnest money is forfeited unless the binder expressly provides that it is to be refunded.

Bona fide Made in good faith; good, valid, without fraud; such as a *bona fide* offer.

Breach The breaking of law, or failure of a duty, either by omission or commission; the failure to perform, without legal excuse, any promise that forms a part or the whole of a contract.

Broker, Real Estate Any person, partnership, association, or corporation that, for a compensation or valuable consideration, sells or offers for sale, buys or offers to buy, or negotiates the purchase or sale or exchange of real estate, or rents or offers to rent, any real estate or the improvements thereon for others. Most state laws require that agents work under the direction of a licensed real estate broker.

Glossary

Caveat Emptor   The Latin phrase literally means "Let the buyer beware." Under this doctrine, the buyer is duty bound to examine the property being purchased and assumes conditions that are readily ascertainable upon view.

Certificate of Title   A certificate issued by a title company or a written opinion rendered by an attorney that says the seller has good marketable and insurable title to the property that he is offering for sale. A certificate of title offers no protection against any hidden defects in the title that an examination of the records could not reveal. The issuer of a certificate of title is liable only for damages due to negligence. The protection offered a homeowner under a certificate of title is not as great as that offered in a title insurance policy.

Chain of Title   A history of conveyances and encumbrances affecting the title to a particular real property.

Chapter 7   Individual or business liquidation under Federal Bankruptcy Code.

Chapter 11   Business reorganization under the Federal Bankruptcy Code.

Chapter 12   Reorganization for farmers under the Federal Bankruptcy Code.

Chapter 13   Relief available under the Federal Bankruptcy Code in which a debtor retains possession of his or her property while making payments to creditors under a court approved plan.

Collateral Estoppel   Prior judgment from a lawsuit between parties on a different cause of action that bars relitigation of those matters in a subsequent lawsuit.

Chattels   Items of moveable personal property, such as animals, household furnishings, money, jewelry, motor vehicles, and all other items which are not permanently affixed to real property and which can be transferred from one place to another.

Closing Costs   The numerous expenses which buyers and sellers normally incur to complete a transaction in the transfer of ownership of real estate. These costs are in addition to the price of the property and are items prepaid at the closing day. Typical closing costs include fees for recording, attorneys, title insurance, appraisals, surveys, inspections, and commissions, to name a few. The agreement of sale negotiated previously between the buyer and the seller may state in writing who will pay each of the above costs. Most of these items are negotiable, but in some states it may be mandated that either the buyer or the seller pay for certain items. For example, in Michigan the seller must pay what is known as the state transfer tax unless it is expressly stated otherwise in the contract.

Closing Day   The day on which the formalities of a real estate sale are concluded. The certificate of title, abstract, and deed are generally prepared for the closing by an attorney, and this cost charged to the buyer. The buyer signs the mortgage, and closing costs are paid. The final closing merely confirms the original agreement reached in the agreement of sale.

Glossary

Cloud on Title An outstanding claim or encumbrance that adversely affects the marketability of title.

Collateral Security A separate obligation attached to a contract to guarantee its performance; the transfer of property or of other contracts or valuables to ensure the performance of a principal agreement or obligation.

Commission Money paid to a real estate agent or broker by the seller as compensation for finding a buyer and completing the sale. Usually it is a percentage of the sale price ranging anywhere from 6 to 7 percent on single family houses and 10 percent on land.

Condominium Individual ownership of a dwelling unit and an individual interest in the common areas and facilities which serve the multiunit project.

Consideration Something of value, usually money, that is the inducement of a contract. Any right, interest, property, or benefit accruing to one party; any forbearance, detriment, loss, or responsibility given, suffered, or undertaken may constitute a consideration that will sustain a contract.

Conventional Mortgage A mortgage loan not insured by HUD or guaranteed by the Veterans' Administration. It is subject to conditions established by the lending institution and state statutes. The mortgage rates may vary with different institutions and between states.

Conversion Clause A provision in some ARMs that allows you to change an ARM to a fixed-rate loan, usually after the first adjustment period. The new fixed rate will be set at current rates, and there may be a charge for the conversion feature.

Cooperative Housing An apartment building or a group of dwellings owned by a corporation, the stockholders of which are the residents of the dwellings. It is operated for their benefit by their elected board of directors. In a cooperative, the corporation or association owns title to the real estate. A resident purchases stock in the corporation that entitles him to occupy a unit in the building or property owned by the cooperative. While the resident does not own the unit, he has an absolute right to occupy this unit for as long as he or she owns the stock.

Covenant An agreement between two or more persons entered into by deed whereby one of the parties promises the performance of certain acts, or that a given state does or shall, or does not or shall not exist.

Credit Report A report detailing the credit history of a prospective borrower that's used to help determine borrower creditworthiness.

Debt An obligation to repay a specified amount at a specified time.

Debt Service The portion of funds required to repay a financial obligation such as a mortgage that includes interest and principal payments.

Glossary

Deed A formal written instrument by which title to real property is transferred from one owner to another. The deed should contain an accurate description of the property being conveyed, should be signed and witnessed according to the laws of the state where the property is located, and should be delivered to the purchaser on the day of closing. There are two parties to a deed: the grantor and the grantee.

Deed in Lieu of Foreclosure The process wherein property owners give title to the lender to avoid a foreclosure.

Deed of Trust Like a mortgage, a security instrument whereby real property is given as security for a debt; however, in a deed of trust there are three parties to the instrument: the borrower, the trustee, and the lender (or beneficiary). In such a transaction, the borrower transfers the legal title for the property to the trustee, who holds the property in trust as security for the payment of the debt to the lender or beneficiary. If the borrower pays the debt as agreed, the deed of trust becomes void. If, however, she defaults in the payment of the debt, the trustee may sell the property at a public sale under the terms of the deed of trust. In most jurisdictions where the deed of trust is in force, the borrower is subject to having her property sold without benefit of legal proceedings. A few states have begun in recent years to treat the deed of trust like a mortgage.

Default Failure to make mortgage payments as agreed upon in a commitment based on the terms and at the designated time set forth in the mortgage or deed of trust. It is the mortgagor's responsibility to remember the due date and send the payment prior to the due date, not after. Generally, 30 days after the due date, if payment is not received, the mortgage is in default. In the event of default, the mortgage may give the lender the right to accelerate payments, take possession and receive rents, and start foreclosure. Defaults may also come about by the failure to observe other conditions in the mortgage or deed of trust.

Default Judgment Judgment entered in a lawsuit when a defendant has failed to enter a plea or otherwise defend himself.

Discount Points (or Points) Points are an upfront fee paid to the lender at the time you get your loan. Each point equals 1 percent of your total loan amount. Points and interest rates are inherently connected: in general, the more points you pay, the lower the interest rate you get. However, the more points you pay, the more cash you need up front, since points are paid in cash at closing.

Documentary Stamps A state tax, in the form of stamps, required on deeds and mortgages when real estate title passes from one owner to another. The amount of stamps required varies with each state.

Down Payment The amount of money to be paid by the purchaser to the seller upon the signing of the agreement of sale. The agreement of sale will refer to the

Glossary

down payment amount and will acknowledge receipt of the down payment. Down payment is the difference between the sales price and maximum mortgage amount. The down payment may not be refundable if the purchaser fails to buy the property without good cause. If the purchaser wants the down payment to be refundable, she should insert a clause in the agreement of sale specifying the conditions under which the deposit will be refunded, if the agreement does not already contain such clause. If the seller cannot deliver good title, the agreement of sale usually requires the seller to return the down payment and to pay interest and expenses incurred by the purchaser.

Duress Unlawful constraint exercised upon a person, whereby the person is forced to perform some act or to sign an instrument or document against his or her will.

Earnest Money The deposit money given to the seller or his agent by the potential buyer upon the signing of the agreement of sale to show that he is serious about buying a house or any other type of real property. If the sale goes through, the earnest money is applied against the down payment. If the sale does not go through, the earnest money will be forfeited or lost unless the binder or offer to purchase expressly provides that it is refundable.

Economic Life The period over which a property may be profitably utilized or the period over which a property will yield a return on the investment, over and above the economic or ground rent due to its land.

Economic Obsolescence Impairment of desirability or useful life arising from economic forces, such as changes in optimum land use, legislative enactments that restrict or impair property rights, and changes in supply and demand relationships.

Eminent Domain The superior right to property subsisting in every sovereign state to take private property for public use upon the payment of just compensation. This power is often conferred upon public service corporations that perform quasi-public functions, such as providing public utilities. In every case, the owner whose property is taken must be justly compensated according to fair market values in the prevailing area.

Encroachment An obstruction, building, or part of a building that intrudes beyond a legal boundary onto neighboring private or public land, or a building extending beyond the building line.

Encumbrance A legal right or interest in land that affects a good or clear title and diminishes the land's value. It can take numerous forms, such as zoning ordinances, easement rights, claims, mortgages, liens, charges, a pending legal action, unpaid taxes, or restrictive covenants. An encumbrance does not legally prevent transfer of the property to another. A title search is all that is usually

Glossary

done to reveal the existence of such encumbrances, and it is up to the buyer to determine whether she wants to purchase with the encumbrance, or what can be done to remove it

Equity The value of a homeowner's unencumbered interest in real estate. Equity is computed by subtracting from the property's fair market value the total of the unpaid mortgage balance and any outstanding liens or other debts against the property. A homeowner's equity increases as he or she pays off the mortgage or as the property appreciates in value. When the mortgage and all other debts against the property are paid in full, the homeowner has 100 percent equity in the property.

Escheat The reverting of property to the state by reason of failure of persons legally entitled to hold it, or when heirs capable of inheriting are lacking the ability to do so.

Escrow Funds paid by one party to another (the escrow agent) to hold until the occurrence of a specified event, after which the funds are released to a designated individual. In FHA mortgage transactions, an escrow account usually refers to the funds a mortgagor pays the lender at the time of the periodic mortgage payments. The money is held in a trust fund, provided by the lender for the buyer. Such funds should be adequate to cover yearly anticipated expenditures for mortgage insurance premiums, taxes, hazard insurance premiums, and special assessments.

Estate The degree, quantum, nature, and extent of interest that one has in real property.

Estoppel A party prevented by his own actions from claiming a right to the detriment of a second party when the second party did some act in reliance on the first party's actions. An estoppel arises when one is forbidden by law to speak against his own action or deed.

Execute To perform what is required to give validity to a legal document. To execute a document, for example, means to sign it so that it becomes fully enforceable by law.

Fee Simple The largest estate a person can have in real estate. Denotes totality of ownership, unlimited in point of time, as in perpetual.

Fiduciary A person to whom property is entrusted; a trustee who holds, controls, or manages for another. A real estate agent is said to have a fiduciary responsibility and relationship with a client.

Financial Distress The events that lead up to the declaration of bankruptcy by a business.

Fixed Rate An interest rate that is fixed for the term of the loan.

Glossary

Fixed-Rate Loans Fixed-rate loans have interest rates that do not change over the life of the loan. As a result, monthly payments for principal and interest are also fixed for the life of the loan. Fixed-rate loans typically have 15-year or 30-year terms. With a fixed-rate loan, you will have predictable monthly mortgage payments for as long as you have the loan.

Foreclosure A legal term applied to any of the various methods of enforcing payment of the debt secured by a mortgage, or deed of trust, by taking and selling the mortgaged property and depriving the mortgagor of possession.

Forfeiture Clause A clause in a lease enabling the landlord to terminate the lease and remove a tenant when the latter defaults in payment of rent or any other obligation under the lease.

Freehold An interest in real estate of not less than a life estate; either a fee simple estate or a life estate.

Functional Obsolescence An impairment of the desirability of a property arising from its being out of date with respect to design and style, capacity and utility in relation to site, lack of modern facilities, and the like.

General Warranty Deed A deed that conveys not only all the grantor's interests in and title to the property to the grantee, but also warrants that if the title is defective or has a "cloud" on it (such as mortgage claims, tax liens, title claims, judgments, or mechanic's liens against it) the grantee may hold the grantor liable.

Good Faith Estimate Written estimate of the settlement costs the borrower will likely have to pay at closing. Under the Real Estate Settlement Procedures Act (RESPA), the lender is required to provide this disclosure to the borrower within three days of receiving a loan application.

Grace Period Period of time during which a loan payment may be made after its due date without incurring a late penalty. The grace period is specified as part of the terms of the loan in the Note.

Grantee That party in the deed who is the buyer or recipient; the person to whom the real estate is conveyed.

Grantor That party in the deed who is the seller or giver; the person who conveys the real estate.

Hazard Insurance Protects against damages caused to property by fire, windstorms, and other common hazards.

Homestead Real property owned by a person under special legal restrictions and exemptions from claims of creditors under the Constitution.

HUD U.S. Department of Housing and Urban Development. The Office of Housing and Federal Housing Administration within HUD insures home mortgage loans made by lenders and sets minimum standards for such homes.

Glossary

Implied Warranty or Covenant A guaranty of assurance the law supplies in an agreement, even though the agreement itself does not express the guaranty or assurance.

Interest A charge paid for borrowing money. (See mortgage note.)

Interest Rate Cap Consumer safeguards that limit the amount the interest rate on an ARM loan can change in an adjustment interval and/or over the life of the loan. For example, if the per-period cap is 1 percent and the current rate is 5 percent, then the newly adjusted rate must fall between 4 percent and 6 percent, regardless of actual changes in the index.

Joint Tenancy Property held by two or more persons together with the right of survivorship. While the doctrine of survivorship has been abolished with respect to most joint tenancies, the tenancy by the entirety retains the doctrine of survivorship in content.

Judgment The decision or sentence of a court of law as the result of proceedings instituted therein for the redress of an injury. A judgment declaring that one individual is indebted to another individual, when properly docketed, creates a lien on the real property of the judgment debtor.

Lease A species of contract, written or oral, between the owner of real estate, the landlord, and another person, the tenant, covering the conditions upon which the tenant may possess, occupy, and use the real estate.

Lessee A person who leases property from another person, usually the landlord.

Lessor The owner or person who rents or leases property to a tenant or lessee; the landlord.

Lien A claim by one person on the property of another as security for money owed. Such claims may include obligations not met or satisfied, judgments, unpaid taxes, materials, or labor.

Loan Application An initial statement of personal and financial information required to apply for a loan.

Loan Application Fee Fee charged by a lender to cover the initial costs of processing a loan application. The fee may include the cost of obtaining a property appraisal, a credit report, and a lock-in fee, or other closing costs incurred during the process, or the fee may be in addition to these charges.

Loan Origination Fee Fee charged by a lender to cover administrative costs of processing a loan.

Loan-to-Value Ratio (LTV) The percentage of the loan amount to the appraised value (or the sales price, whichever is less) of the property.

Lock or Lock-In A lender's guarantee of an interest rate for a set period of time. The time period is usually that between loan application approval and loan closing. The lock-in protects one against rate increases during that time.

Glossary

Marketable Title   A title that is free and clear of objectionable liens, clouds, or other title defects. A title that enables an owner to sell his or her property freely to others and that others will accept without objection.

Market Value   The amount for which a property would sell if put upon the open market and sold in the manner by which property is ordinarily sold in the community in which the property is situated. The highest price estimated in terms of money that a buyer would be warranted in paying and a seller would be justified in accepting, provided both parties were fully informed, acted intelligently and voluntarily, and, furthermore, that all the rights and benefits inherent in or attributable to the property were included in the transfer.

Meeting of Minds   A mutual intention of two persons to enter into a contract affecting their legal status based on agreed upon terms.

Mortgage   A lien or claim against real property given by the buyer to the lender as security for money borrowed. Under government insured or loan guarantee provisions, the payments may include escrow amounts covering taxes, hazard insurance, water charges, and special assessments. Mortgages generally run from 10 to 30 years, during which the loan is to be paid off.

Mortgagee   The one receiving a mortgage (usually a financial institution). The lender.

Mortgagor   The one granting a mortgage on his or her property. The borrower.

Mortgage Commitment   A written notice from the bank or other lending institution saying it will advance mortgage funds in a specified amount to enable a buyer to purchase a house.

Mortgage Insurance Premium   The payment made by a borrower to the lender for transmittal to HUD to help defray the cost of the FHA mortgage insurance program and to provide a reserve fund to protect lenders against loss in insured mortgage transactions. In FHA insured mortgages, this represents an annual rate of one-half of 1 percent paid by the mortgagor on a monthly basis.

Mortgage Note   A written agreement to repay a loan. The agreement is secured by a mortgage, serves as proof of an indebtedness, and states the manner in which it shall be paid. The note states the actual amount of the debt that the mortgage secures and renders the mortgagor personally responsible for repayment.

Mortgage (Open-End)   A mortgage with a provision that permits borrowing additional money in the future without refinancing the loan or paying additional financing charges. Open-end provisions often limit such borrowing to no more than would raise the balance to the original loan figure.

Negative Amortization   A loan payment schedule in which the outstanding principal balance of a loan goes up rather than down because the payments do not

Glossary

cover the full amount of interest due. The monthly shortfall in payment is added to the unpaid principal balance of the loan.

Non-Assumption Clause A statement in a mortgage contract forbidding the assumption of the mortgage by another borrower without the prior approval of the lender.

Note An instrument of credit given to attest a debt; a written promise to pay money, which may or may not accompany a mortgage or other security agreement.

Offer A proposal, oral or written, to buy a piece of property at a specified price with specified terms and conditions.

Option The exclusive right to purchase or lease a property at a stipulated price or rent within a specified period of time.

Personal Property Moveable property that is not by definition real property and includes tangible property such as moneys, goods, chattels, as well as debts and claims.

Per Diem Interest Interest calculated per day. (Depending on the day of the month on which closing takes place, you will have to pay interest from the date of closing to the end of the month. Your first mortgage payment will probably be due the first day of the following month.)

PITI Abbreviation for principal, interest, taxes, and insurance, the components of a monthly mortgage payment.

Points Sometimes referred to as "discount points." A point is 1 percent of the amount of the mortgage loan. For example, if a loan is for $250,000, one point is $2,500. Points are charged by a lender to raise the yield on a loan at a time when money is tight, interest rates are high, and there is a legal limit to the interest rate that can be charged on a mortgage. Buyers are prohibited from paying points on HUD or Veterans' Administration guaranteed loans. (Sellers can pay them, however.) On a conventional mortgage, points may be paid by either buyer or seller, or split between them.

Prepayment Payment of mortgage loan, or part of it, before due date. Mortgage agreements often restrict the right of prepayment either by limiting the amount that can be prepaid in any one year or charging a penalty for prepayment. The Federal Housing Administration does not permit such restrictions in FHA insured mortgages.

Principal The basic element of the loan as distinguished from the interest and mortgage insurance premium. In other words, principal is the amount upon which interest is paid. The word also means one who appoints an agent to act for and on behalf of; the person bound by an agent's authorized contract.

Glossary

Property The term used to describe the rights and interests a person has in lands, chattels, and other determinate things.

Purchase Agreement An offer to purchase that has been accepted by the seller and has become a binding contract.

Quit Claim Deed A deed that transfers whatever interest the maker of the deed may have in the particular parcel of land. A quit claim deed is often given to clear the title when the grantor's interest in a property is questionable. By accepting such a deed, the buyer assumes all the risks. Such a deed makes no warranties as to the title, but simply transfers to the buyer whatever interest the grantor has. (See deed.)

Real Estate Agent An intermediary who buys and sells real estate for a company, firm, or individual and is compensated on a commission basis. The agent does not have title to the property, but generally has a fiduciary obligation to represent the owner.

Real Estate Investment Trust (REIT) An entity that allows a very large number of investors to participate in the purchase of real estate, but as passive investors. The investors do not buy directly, but instead purchase shares in the REIT that owns the real estate investment. REITs are fairly common with the advent of mutual funds and can be purchased for as little as $10 per share, and sometimes less.

Real Property Land and buildings and anything that may be permanently attached to them.

Recording The placing of a copy of a document in the proper books in the office of the Register of Deeds so that a public record will be made of it.

Redemption The right that an owner-mortgagor or one claiming under him has after execution of the mortgage to recover back his title to the mortgaged property by paying the mortgage debt plus interest and any other costs or penalties imposed prior to the occurrence of a valid foreclosure. The payment discharges the mortgage and places the title back as it was at the time the mortgage was executed.

Reinstate The payment of money sufficient to cure all amounts past due, including reasonable fees and costs incurred as a result of a default on a loan.

Refinancing The process of the same mortgagor paying off one loan with the proceeds from another loan.

Reformation The correction of a deed or other instrument by reason of a mutual mistake of the parties involved or because of the mistake of one party caused by the fraud or inequitable conduct of the other party.

Release The giving up or abandoning of a claim or right to the person against whom the claim exists or against whom the right is to be exercised or enforced.

Glossary

Release of Lien The discharge of certain property from the lien of a judgment, mortgage, or claim.

Rent A compensation, either in money, provisions, chattels, or labor, received by the owner of real estate from a tenant for the occupancy of the premises.

Rescission of Contract The abrogating or annulling of a contract; the revocation or repealing of contract by mutual consent of the parties to the contract, or for other causes as recognized by law.

Restrictive Covenants Private restrictions limiting the use of real property. Restrictive covenants are created by deed and may run with the land, thereby binding all subsequent purchasers of the land, or may be deemed personal and binding only between the original seller and buyer. The determination whether a covenant runs with the land or is personal is governed by the language of the covenant, the intent of the parties, and the law in the state where the land is situated. Restrictive covenants that run with the land are encumbrances and may affect the value and marketability of title. Restrictive covenants may limit the density of buildings per acre; regulate size, style, or price range of buildings to be erected; or prevent particular businesses from operating or minority groups from owning or occupying homes in a given area. This latter discriminatory covenant is unconstitutional and has been declared unenforceable by the U.S. Supreme Court.

Revocation The recall of a power or authority conferred, or the vacating of an instrument previously made.

Right of Survivorship Granted to two joint owners who purchase using that particular buying method. Stipulates that one gets full rights and becomes the sole owner of the property upon the death of the other. Right of survivorship is the fundamental difference between acquiring property as joint owners and as tenants in common.

Special Assessment A legal charge against real estate by a public authority to pay the cost of public improvements, such as for the opening, grading, and guttering of streets, the construction of sidewalks and sewers, or the installation of streetlights or other such items to be used for public purposes.

Special Lien A lien that binds a specified piece of property, unlike a general lien, which is levied against all one's assets. It creates a right to retain something of value belonging to another person as compensation for labor, material, or money expended in that person's behalf. In some localities it is called *particular lien* or *specific lien*.

Special Warranty Deed A deed in which the grantor conveys title to the grantee and agrees to protect the grantee against title defects or claims asserted by the

Glossary

grantor and those persons whose right to assert a claim against the title arose during the period the grantor held title to the property. In a special warranty deed the grantor guarantees to the grantee that she has done nothing during the time she held title to the property which has, or which might in the future, impair the grantee's title.

Specific Performance   A remedy in the court of equity whereby the defendant may be compelled to do whatever he has agreed to do in a contract executed by him.

Statute   A law established by the act of the legislative powers; an act of the legislature; the written will of the legislature solemnly expressed according to the forms necessary to constitute it as the law provides.

Subdivision   A tract of land divided into smaller parcels of land, or lots, usually for the purpose of constructing new houses.

Sublease   An agreement whereby one person who has leased land from the owner rents out all or a portion of the premises for a period ending prior to the expiration of the original lease.

Subordination Clause   A clause in a mortgage or lease stating that one who has a prior claim or interest agrees that his or her interest or claim shall be secondary or subordinate to a subsequent claim, encumbrance, or interest.

Survivorship   The distinguishing feature of a tenancy by the entirety, by which, on the death of one spouse, the surviving spouse acquires full ownership.

Tax   As applied to real estate, an enforced charge imposed on persons, property, or income, to be used to support the state. The governing body in turn utilizes the funds in the best interests of the general public.

Tax Deed   A deed given where property has been purchased at public sale because of the owner's nonpayment of taxes.

Tax Sale   A sale of property for nonpayment of taxes assessed against it.

Tenant   One who holds or possesses land or tenements by any kind of title, either in fee, for life, for years, or at will. The term is most commonly used for one who has, under lease, the temporary use and occupation of real property that belongs to another person or persons. The tenant is the lessee.

Time is of the Essence   A phrase meaning that time is of crucial value and vital importance and that failure to fulfill time deadlines will be considered to be a failure to perform the contract.

Title   As generally used, the rights of ownership and possession of particular property. In real estate usage, title may refer to the instruments or documents by which a right of ownership is established (title documents), or it may refer to the ownership interest one has in the real estate.

Glossary

Title Insurance   Protects lenders or homeowners against loss of their interest in property due to legal defects in title. Title insurance may be issued to a mortgagee's title policy. Insurance benefits will be paid only to the "named insured" in the title policy, so it is important that an owner purchase an "owner's title policy" if he desires the protection of title insurance.

Title Search or Examination   A check of the title records, generally at the local courthouse, to make sure the buyer is purchasing a house from the legal owner and there are no liens, overdue special assessments, or other claims or outstanding restrictive covenants filed in the record that would adversely affect the marketability or value of title.

Trust   A relationship under which one person, the trustee, holds legal title to property for the benefit of another person, the trust beneficiary.

Trustee   A party who is given legal responsibility to hold property in the best interests of or "for the benefit of" another. The trustee is a person who is placed in a position of responsibility for another, a responsibility enforceable in a court of law.

Truth-in-Lending Act   Federal law requiring written disclosure of the terms of a mortgage (including the APR and other charges) by a lender to a borrower after application. Also requires the right to a rescission period.

Underwriting   In mortgage lending, the process of determining the risks involved in a particular loan and establishing suitable terms and conditions for the loan.

Unimproved   As relating to land, vacant or lacking in essential appurtenant improvements required to serve a useful purpose.

Useful Life   The period of time over which a commercial property can be depreciated for tax purposes. A property's useful life is also referred to as its economic life.

Usury   Charging a higher rate of interest on a loan than is allowed by law.

Valid   Having force or binding forces; legally sufficient and authorized by law.

Valuation   The act or process of estimating value; the amount of estimated value.

Value   Ability to command goods, including money, in exchange; the quantity of goods, including money, that should be commanded or received in exchange for the item valued. As applied to real estate, value is the present worth of all the rights to future benefits arising from ownership.

Variance   An exception to a zoning ordinance granted to meet certain specific needs, usually given on an individual case by case basis.

Void   That which is unenforceable; having no force or effect.

Waiver   Renunciation, disclaiming, or surrender of some claim, right, or prerogative.

Glossary

Warranty Deed A deed that transfers ownership of real property and in which the grantor guarantees that the title is free and clear of any and all encumbrances.

Zoning Ordinances The acts of an authorized local government to establish building codes and set forth regulations for property land usage.

Index

Index

Index

Index

Possession, 114, 150, 158–159
Pre-approval letter, 102
Pre-qualification letter, 111
Price, 41–43, 45
Professional legal services, 47–48
Professional moving company, 161
Profile of Home Buyers and Sellers, 61
Promissory note, 55, 183–184
Property condition disclosure, 50–51, 176–177
Prorations, 116–117, 153
Protection from future litigation, 133–134
Purchase agreement, 108–119
  agreement of parties, 119
  attorney's fees, 118
  broker's fees, 114
  casualty loss, 117
  closing, 114
  consult your attorney, 119
  default, 117
  dispute resolution, 117
  earnest money, 111
  escrow, 118
  federal tax requirements, 119
  financing, 111
  parties, 109
  possession, 114–115
  property, 109–110
  property condition, 113
  prorations, 116–117
  sales price, 110–111
  sample form, 170–175
  seller's representations, 118–119
  settlement and other expenses, 116
  signature/witness, 106–107
  special provisions, 116
  survey, 112–113
  title policy, 112

Quit Claim deed, 57–58, 187

Real estate agent
  CMA, 39
  commission, 74
  discount brokerage services, 74–77
  fee-for-service agents, 75–77
  MLS, 77–79
  perceived *vs.* real costs, 80–81
  reducing the commission, 79–80
Real estate commission, 74
Real estate forms, 46–58, 169–187
  lead based paint disclosure, 51–52, 178
  loan assumption addendum, 52–53, 181
  notice of termination, 56, 185
  promissory note, 55, 183–184
  property condition disclosure, 50–51, 176–177
  quit claim deed, 57–58, 187
  residential sales contract, 49–50, 170–175

Real estate forms (*Cont.*):
  seller financing addendum, 53–55, 182
  third party financing addendum, 52, 179–180
  warranty deed, 56–57, 186
Real estate magazines, 66
Real property, 110
Refreshments, 90
Relocation package, 161
Repairs, 12–35. *See also* Exterior home preparations; Interior home preparations
Repayment of debt, 54
Replacement cost method, 138
Representations, 118–119
Residential sales contract, 49–50, 170–175.
  See Purchase agreement
Roof repair/replacement, 21–22

Sales comparison method, 138
Sales price, 41–43, 45
Seller carry back, 53
Seller financing, 43
Seller financing addendum, 53–55, 182
Seller's representations, 118–119
Sensory-rich experience, 86–90
Setting the price, 41–43
Settlement charges, 116
Settlement statement, 150–153, 154–155
Shingles, 22
Showing your house. *See* Home presentation
Siding, 20
Sight, 87
Smell, 87–88
Smile, 93
Snack, 90
Sound, 88–89
State transfer tax, 47, 116
Strategic marketing, 61–72
  classified ads, 63–65
  flyer, 71–72
  information box, 68–69
  Internet marketing, 66–67
  marketing budget, 62–63
  networking, 70–71
  newspapers, 63–65, 67
  open house, 69–70
  real estate magazines, 66
  yard sign, 67–68
Subject to clauses, 102–105
Survey, 112–113
Symphony Homes, 167–168
Symphony Homes Web site, 67

Taste, 90
Tax information, 148
Terminology (glossary), 188–208
thevalueplay.com, 165–166
Third party financing addendum, 52, 179–180
Tires, 19